I Loved You Like That!

Winter, Season of the Heart

MGM Meddis

Volume 4

Dedication Page:

To those who have loved fiercely and fought valiantly for that love—across valleys and mountains, through storms and sunshine. This story is a tribute to the enduring power of love, to its ability to inspire growth, foster resilience, and transcend time.

To our ancestors, whose stories and sacrifices have woven the rich tapestry of our present, and to the future generations, who will carry these threads forward, crafting their own tales of love and legacy. May you always find strength in your roots and light in each other, guiding you through the seasons of your hearts.

And to the natural world, our eternal muse and teacher, reminding us of the beauty in change, the wisdom in cycles, and the promise of renewal. May we walk gently upon this earth, ever mindful of the legacy we leave behind.

This book is dedicated to all who believe in the transformative power of love, to those who understand that while seasons change, the heart's capacity for love remains boundless.

May you find your story within these pages and be inspired to weave your own tapestry of love and legacy.

Introduction.

In the whispering valleys of Wales, where legends sleep beneath the hills and history breathes through the stone of ancient castles, a tale of love as enduring as the land itself unfolds. I LOVED YOU LIKE THAT! Winter, Seasons of the Heart. Invites you on a journey through time, where the passions of the heart collide with the tumult of history, weaving a story that transcends the ages.

This is not just a love story. It is an odyssey of two souls, Charles, and Sognia, bound by a love that defies societal constraints, battles the forces of change, and emerges, not unscathed, but more beautiful for having braved the storm. Set against the backdrop of Wales's verdant landscapes and tumultuous history, their tale is a testament to the power of love to inspire, to challenge, and to endure.

From the first bloom of love in the shadow of Snowdonia to the legacy left in its wake, Charles and Sognia's journey is a mirror to our own reflecting the myriad ways in which love shapes, molds, and ultimately defines us. Through letters penned by moonlight, poems whispered against the backdrop of revolution, and melodies that bind generations, their story is a beacon for all who have dared to love deeply.

As you turn these pages, allow yourself to be transported to a world where love is both a sanctuary and a battlefield, where every Season brings its own challenges and joys, and where the legacy of love is the most precious inheritance of all.

"Seasons of the Heart" is more than a narrative; it is an invitation to explore the depths of your own heart, to rediscover the bonds that tie us to each other and to the past, and to remember that in the end, love is the greatest journey of all.

Welcome to a story that you will never forget—a story that will linger in your heart long after the final page is turned.

Synopsis.

In the heart of Wales, amidst its verdant hills and shadowed valleys, I LOVED YOU LIKE THAT! Winter, Seasons of the Heart. Tells the epic love story of Sognia, a spirited miner's daughter with an artist's heart, and Charles, a poet whose words bear the power of revolution. Their love, born under the expansive skies of a country on the brink of cultural renaissance, becomes a beacon for their community, a symbol of hope amid the tumult of the early 20th century.

As the Welsh Revival stirs the souls of their countrymen, calling forth a rebirth of language, culture, and identity, Charles and Sognia find themselves at the crossroads of personal passion and national pride. Their love, tender and fierce, faces trials by societal norms, family expectations, and the very tides of history that sweep through their homeland.

Sognia, with her weaver's hands, crafts tapestries that tell the tales of Wales, weaving her love for Charles into every thread, while Charles, with his bard's soul, composes verses that echo the couple's devotion and the stirring spirit of their time. Together, they engage in the struggles and triumphs of their community, embodying the resurgence of Welsh identity through their unwavering commitment to each other and their shared values.

But love, like the seasons, changes and evolves. "I Loved You Like That!" navigates the couple's journey through the blossoming of their romance in spring, the warmth and challenges of summer, the reflections and transformations of autumn, and the introspective closeness of winter.

Each season brings its own trials and triumphs, shaping Charles and Sognia in the fires of adversity and the soothing balm of joy.

Through letters, poems, songs, and recipes, the narrative delves deep into the couple's inner world, offering a rich tapestry of emotional landscapes that resonate with the power of heritage and the timeless nature of love itself. As Charles and Sognia story unfolds, it becomes clear that their love is not merely their own, but a legacy passed down through generations, influencing and shaping the lives of those around them.

At its core, " I Loved You Like That!" is a celebration of the enduring human spirit, a homage to the beauty of the Welsh land and culture, and a testament to the profound impact of love on the course of our lives.

It invites readers to witness the remarkable journey of a couple whose love story becomes a symbol of resilience, identity, and the unbreakable bonds of the heart.

This is a narrative that not only captivates but also inspires, leaving an indelible mark on the hearts of those who journey through its pages.

Beginning Poem:

"When First We Tread"

When first we tread upon the verdant spring,
Our hearts as wild as streams that freely flow,
We knew not what the turning seasons bring,
Or how the seeds of love in time would grow.

Beneath the vast expanse of azure skies,
Our souls did dance, unbridled, bold, and free.
In every dawn, a new world to surmise,
Together bound, yet in our spirits, we.

The journey long, through summer's fervent blaze,
And autumn's gold, to winter's silent night,
Has taught our hearts to navigate the maze,
And in the dark to find each other's light.

So, let this verse, a doorway be, to start,
The tale of how love dances, heart to heart.

Her Sonnet:

The Stillness of First Snow

In the quiet hush of snow's gentle fall,
Our world lies serene, in white draped and still,
Each flake, a whispered love, at winter's call,
Blankets our life, in the chill's tender thrill.

I loved thee as the first snow loves the night,
Softly, in silence, with grace pure and fair,
In the cold's embrace, we found warmth, alight,
A love so deep, none other could compare.

As seasons turn, and years fade into past,
Our hearts remain steadfast, through frost and thaw,
In winter's grip, our love is held fast,
A testament to what the heart saw.

For in the quiet of snowfall's embrace,
Our love found its time, its eternal place.

Her Love Letter:

Dearest, in the winter of our lives, amidst the quiet beauty of the world swathed in its virginal white, I find myself reflecting on the profound journey of our love. Like the first snowfall, silent and profound, our affection has blanketed the landscape of our existence, transforming the mundane into the extraordinary.

In the stillness that accompanies the snow's descent, I see the quiet force of our love. It has been a steadfast companion through the vicissitudes of life, offering solace in moments of turmoil and amplifying joy in times of happiness. Our love, much like the winter's snow, has a way of smoothing the rough edges of the world, offering a softening lens through which we view our shared experiences.

As we face the winter of our lives, I am comforted by the endurance of our love. It has been a source of strength, a beacon that guides us through the darkest nights. Our love is a quiet force, one that resonates in the silent moments, in the shared glances, and in the comfort of our intertwined hands.

I cherish the legacy of our love, the way it continues to shape our existence, offering a sense of belonging, a reservoir of strength, and an ever-present comfort. As we navigate the remaining chapters of our journey together, I am grateful for the indelible mark your love has left on my heart, echoing through the silence and the noise, forever a part of the melody of our existence.

With all the love that dwells within the winter of my heart, Yours, forever and always. Sognia

His Sonnet:

In Winter's Embrace

As winter cloaks the world in silent white,
Your love, the flame that warms the coldest night.
With every snowflake's fall, my heart takes flight,
For in your eyes, I find my guiding light.

Our journey's seen the seasons come and go,
Yet here we stand, as time itself bows low.
In love's quiet strength, our spirits glow,
A bond that time nor tide can overthrow.

The silent snow, our love's pure reflection,
A canvas broad for our affection's projection.
In winter's quiet, we find our direction,
In each other's heart, our perfect section.

Through life's winter, our love's the steadfast dawn,
A promise kept, forever to live on.

His Love Letter:

My Dearest, as the world outside our window submits to the silent dominion of winter, I am reminded of the profound journey we have embarked upon together. Our love, much like the season's first snowfall, is a gentle yet transformative force that has shaped the landscape of our lives.

In the tranquility of this season, I find a deep sense of gratitude for the love we share. It is a love that has weathered the storms of life, standing resilient against the winds of change. As the snow blankets the earth, so has your love enveloped me, providing comfort, warmth, and an unshakeable sense of belonging.

As we embrace the winter of our existence, I am moved by the enduring nature of our connection. Our love has been a quiet force, guiding us through every challenge, illuminating our darkest days, and enriching our happiest moments. It is in the shared silences, the subtle glances, and the simple touches that our love speaks its most profound truths.

The legacy of our love is etched into the very essence of my being. It is a legacy that resonates with the quiet force of love's enduring presence, offering strength, solace, and a profound sense of unity. As we continue on this journey, hand in hand, I am filled with a sense of awe for the depth and breadth of our love.

Your love is the melody that accompanies me through the silence and the noise, an eternal symphony that celebrates the beauty of our shared existence. As we face the remaining chapters of our story, I do so with a heart overflowing with love for you, grateful for every moment, every memory, and every breath we share.

With all the love that has blossomed in the winter of my soul, Yours, now and always, through all seasons of life. Charles

His Sonnet:

"And I loved you like that with the calm of the winter's embrace, finding peace in the silence, our love the warmth amidst the cold."

The Calm of Winter's Embrace

In winter's calm, our hearts found peace so rare,
A silence deep, where truest loves declare.
Amidst the cold, our warmth did none compare,
Your love, the fire in frosty air so fair.

I loved you thus, with all the winter's grace,
Our souls entwined in cold's serene embrace.
Through silent nights and frost's gentle trace,
Our love, a flame that time cannot erase.

The quiet peace, where whispers of love resound,
In winter's grip, our steadfast love we found.
A sanctuary where true love is crowned,
In each other, our hearts were truly bound.

For in the calm of winter's embrace so bold,
Our love, the warmth that never grows old.

His Love Letter:

My Dearest, in the hush that winter brings, amidst the tranquil peace of its embrace, our love has been a beacon, a source of warmth and light against the backdrop of the season's cold. With every snowflake that dances in the silent air, I am reminded of the purity and depth of our affection, a love that transcends the chill and brings a soft glow to the coldest of days.

In this season of quietude, our love has been my sanctuary, a peaceful haven where the chaos of the world fades into the background, and all that remains is the profound connection that we share. It is in this silence that our love speaks the loudest, a testament to the strength and durability of the bond that we have forged together.

As we stand amidst the serene beauty of winter, I find myself reflecting on the journey we have taken, the paths we have walked side by side, and the countless ways in which your love has enriched my life. You are the calm in the midst of the storm, the peace that soothes my restless soul, and the warmth that shelters me from the cold.

Our love is a rare and precious gift, a flame that burns brightly in the heart of winter, casting a gentle light that guides us through the darkest nights. It is a love that has grown and deepened with each passing season, a love that offers comfort, joy, and an unshakeable sense of belonging.

As we embrace the quiet beauty of this season, I am filled with gratitude for the love that we share, a love that endures and flourishes in the calm of winter's embrace. You are my heart, my soul, and the very essence of my being. Together, we stand strong against the cold, our love the eternal warmth that sustains us through every season of life.

With all the love that fills my heart in the quiet of the winter night, Yours, always and forever. Charles

2. Her:

"In the longest night, we found the brightness of our love, a beacon shining against the dark, defying the short days and long shadows."

The Longest Night's Light

In longest night, our love did shine so bright,
A beacon 'gainst the dark, in stark contrast,
Defying shadows long, and day's short light,
Our love, a fire that will forever last.

Through shortest days, where shadows stretch and loom,
Our hearts found solace in each other's glow,
Amidst the gloom, our love did bloom and boom,
A steadfast light, no darkness could overthrow.

This love of ours, a lighthouse in the night,
Guiding us through, when hope seemed out of sight.
In love's warm embrace, we found our true might,
Together standing, in love's endless flight.

So here we stand, where dark meets light's embrace,
Our love, the brightest star in darkest space.

Her Love Letter:

My Dearest, as the days grow shorter and the nights stretch into their longest, I find a profound comfort in the enduring brilliance of our love. It shines like a beacon in the darkness, defying the encroaching shadows and the chill that seeks to pervade our bones. Our love, it seems, is made for these times, when the world around us retreats into slumber, and all seems quiet and still.

In this season of long nights, our love has been the light that guides me, a constant and unwavering flame that burns with a warmth and brightness that no shadow can diminish. It is in this light that we find each other, time and time again, our souls reaching across the darkness, finding solace and strength in the glow of our shared affection.

The world may grow cold, and the days may shorten, but in you, I have found an eternal summer, a place where the light of our love chases away any chill. Your presence is my sanctuary, a haven where the lengthening shadows cannot reach, where the darkness is always held at bay by the light of our bond.

As we move through these shortest days and longest nights, let us hold fast to the light of our love, for it is in this brilliance that we find our way. It is a light that not only guides us but also illuminates the path for others, a testament to the strength and beauty of what we have together.

Let us cherish this light, my dearest, for it is rare and precious. In the heart of the longest night, it is our love that shines the brightest, a beacon of hope, warmth, and unwavering devotion that will carry us through to the dawn of a new day.

With all the love that shines brightly in my heart, through the longest night and beyond, Yours, forever and always. Sognia

His Sonnet:

Beacon in the Night

In night's deep realm, where shadows stretch and play,
Our love, a beacon bright, does shine and sway.
Against the dark, our hearts do not dismay,
For in our love, the night turns into day.

The longest night, with you, feels all too brief,
Our love, a flame, burns away all grief.
In its warm glow, we find our sweet relief,
In every shared moment, every shared belief.

This love of ours, against the dark, a shield,
In its bright light, all fears are forced to yield.
Through time's long march, to none shall we concede,
For in our love, we've all that we will need.

So let the night extend, let shadows cast,
In our love's light, we'll hold each other fast.

His Love Letter:

My Beloved, as the world succumbs to the longest night, and the shadows lengthen, reaching into the very corners of our existence, I find an unwavering source of light and warmth in the love that we share. It is a love that defies the short days and the encroaching darkness, a beacon that shines with a resolute and enduring brightness.

In this season of extended shadows and dwindling daylight, our love stands as a testament to the power of light over darkness, of warmth over cold. It is in the glow of our affection that I find my courage, my hope, and my joy. Our love illuminates the path forward, guiding us through the darkness with the promise of dawn's impending return.

As the world outside grows colder and the nights longer, I am reminded of the warmth that resides within, a warmth that emanates from the heart of our bond. It is a warmth that no winter can chill, a light that no shadow can dim. Our love is a fire that burns brighter with each passing day, a source of strength and comfort that sees us through the longest night.

In the quiet and the stillness that this season brings, I find myself reflecting on the depth of our connection, marveling at the light we create together. It is a light that not only guides us but also serves as a beacon for all who navigate their own darkness, a shining example of love's enduring power.

Let us take solace in the brilliance of our love, my dearest, for it is in this light that we find our true selves. Together, we defy the darkness, our bond a declaration of love's triumph over the longest nights. As we move forward, hand in hand, let us carry this light with us, a beacon of hope, love, and unwavering commitment that will guide us through to the dawn.

With all the love that burns brightly in my heart, against the dark, and into the light, Yours, now and forevermore. Charles

His:

"Through the longest night, your love was my light, guiding me through darkness, a promise of the dawn to come."

Dawn's Promised Light

Through longest night, your love, my guiding star,
Illuminates the path where shadows mar.
In darkness deep, where weary spirits are,
Your love's the dawn, no night could ever bar.

Each moment spent in night's embrace, I find,
Your love, a beacon bright, to darkness, blind.
It leads me through, leaves shadowed doubts behind,
In your light, the dawn's promise, intertwined.

So steadfast is your love, through night's long test,
A harbinger of joy, in dark's arrest.
With you, my soul finds peace, and heart finds rest,
In love's light, we are eternally blessed.

For through the night, your love does more than shine,
It promises the dawn, forever mine.

His Love Letter:

My Dearest Heart,

As we journeyed together through the longest night, it was your love that shone like a beacon in the dark, guiding me, comforting me, and promising the dawn to come. In the profound silence and the profound darkness, where time seemed to stand still and the world awaited the first light of morning, your love was a constant source of warmth and light.

Your love, my dearest, has been the lighthouse guiding me through life's darkest nights, a steady and unwavering light that never dims. It has been the promise of dawn in the midst of darkness, a reminder that no night, no matter how long or how dark, can withstand the inevitable arrival of the morning light.

In those moments when the darkness seemed unending, when the night stretched on with no end in sight, your love was the promise of a new day. It was the assurance that, no matter how difficult the journey, the dawn would come, bringing with it light, warmth, and the beauty of a new beginning.

Your love has illuminated my path, dispelled the shadows, and brought color back into my world. It has been my strength and my hope, a constant reminder that, even in the darkest times, there is light, there is love, and there is a reason to keep moving forward.

As we stand now, with the night behind us and the dawn stretching out before us, I am filled with gratitude for the light of your love. You are my dawn, my daybreak, and the promise of all the beautiful mornings to come.

With all the love in my heart, and with the light of your love guiding me, I look forward to the dawn of each new day with you.

Forever and always, your light in the darkness, Yours. Charles

3. Her:

"We watched our breath form clouds in the chilly air, our words visible then gone, like the fleeting moments we cherish and remember."

Breath in the Chilly Air

In chilly air, our breath forms clouds so light,
Words visible, then gone, in winter's kiss.
Like fleeting moments, cherished in our sight,
Each one a memory, we dare not miss.

Together, standing in the cold's embrace,
We speak in puffs of air, our words take flight.
These moments, fragile, time cannot erase,
They dwell in hearts, where love burns ever bright.

As seasons change, and years may come and go,
The warmth of shared breaths in cold air remains.
In every word, in every frosty glow,
Our love's story, in winter's breath, contains.

For in the chill, where breath and words combine,
Our souls connect, in moments so divine.

Her Love Letter:

Dearest Love,

In the crispness of these wintry days, as we watch our breath form clouds in the chilly air, I am reminded of the transient beauty of the moments we share. Our words, visible for an instant before they fade away, are like the precious, fleeting moments that make up the tapestry of our lives together. Each one, though ephemeral, is imprinted upon my heart, cherished and remembered with a fondness that time cannot diminish.

These moments, though as fleeting as our breath in the cold air, hold within them the essence of our journey together. They are the quiet whispers of our love, the gentle laughter that warms the coldest days, and the silent understanding that speaks volumes. In the visible breath of our conversations, in the shared glances that linger in the air between us, our love finds its expression, delicate yet enduring.

As we stand together, watching our breath mingle in the chilly air, I am struck by the beauty of the mundane, the magic in the ordinary. These moments, seemingly insignificant, are the ones that we will look back on with the greatest affection. They are the memories that we will cherish, the stories we will recount with a smile, the silent witnesses to the depth of our connection.

In the cold air, as our words become visible and then disappear, let us remember the impermanence of each moment and the importance of cherishing them. Let us continue to create these fleeting memories, to find joy in the simple act of being together, and to fill the chilly air with the warmth of our love.

With each breath we see and each word we speak, know that my love for you is as constant as the stars, as enduring as the passing of time, & as precious as the fleeting moments we cherish & remember.

Yours, in love and in the beauty of every moment, Yours forever. Sognia

His Sonnet:

Clouds of Breath and Memory

In winter's grip, where chill winds softly blow,
Our breaths, like clouds, in cold air come to show.
Words spoken, seen, then lost in frosty glow,
Like fleeting moments, precious, full of woe.

Each puff of air, a memory we weave,
Invisible threads in the heart's loom cleave.
These moments pass, yet deeply we perceive,
The beauty in what we silently achieve.

Our love, a collection of breaths shared,
In cold, in warmth, in everything dared.
Through visible words, our souls bared,
In fleeting clouds, our deepest hopes declared.

For in the chill, where our warm breaths blend,
We find our love, timeless, without end.

His Love Letter:

My Dearest,

In the chill of the air, as we watch our breath form fleeting clouds, vanishing as quickly as they appear, I am reminded of the ephemeral nature of the moments we share. Yet, in their fleeting existence, these moments capture the essence of our journey together each one cherished, each one a testament to the love we share.

Our words, though temporary in the winter air, are permanent in the warmth of our hearts. They are reminders of the laughter, the joy, and the quiet companionship that define us. Like the breath that escapes in visible puffs, our time together is filled with moments that, though they may disappear from sight, leave a lasting impression on our souls.

In this dance of warmth and cold, of visibility and disappearance, I find a beautiful metaphor for our love. It is a love that, despite the inevitable passing of time, remains constant in its presence and impact. Our love is not measured by the permanence of what can be seen, but by the enduring effect it has on us, the way it shapes our lives and fills our memories with joy.

As we navigate through the chill of life, let us continue to cherish each fleeting moment, each breath in the cold air, each word that hangs momentarily before us. These are the snapshots of our lives together, the small yet profound experiences that, when woven together, create the rich tapestry of our shared existence.

With every breath that forms a cloud in the chilly air, with every word that becomes visible then disappears, know that my love for you is unwavering. It is a love that, like our breath in the cold, may not always be visible, but is always present, always warming, and always cherished.

Here's to all the moments we've shared, and to all the moments yet to come—each one precious, each one a reminder of the love that binds us.

Forever and always, in love and in memory, Yours, Charles

His Reply:

"Each breath, a visible testament to our love, ephemeral yet eternal, captured in the frosty air between us."

His Sonnet: Ephemeral Yet Eternal

Each breath we take, in cold air's frosty sweep,
A testament to love that lies so deep.
Ephemeral, yet eternal, it's a leap,
In frosty air, our love's promise to keep.

Visible in the chill, our love declares,
In puffs of breath, our hearts' enduring tales.
Though fleeting, in this moment, none compares,
To love's soft whisper, in the winter, prevails.

Our words, though gone, in heart remain so clear,
Each breath, a bond, through cold air, draws us near.
Invisible soon, yet forever dear,
Our love's essence, in winter's chill, we cheer.

For in each breath, though ephemeral it seems,
Lies love's eternal flame, beyond dreams.

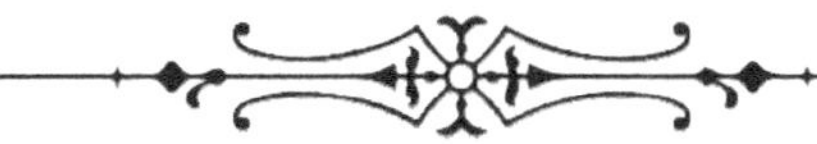

His Love Letter:

My Beloved,

In the stillness of the frosty air, where each breath we share becomes a visible testament to our love, I find a profound beauty in the ephemerality of these moments. They are fleeting, yes, but in their brief existence, they capture the essence of our enduring love. Each cloud of breath, vanishing as quickly as it forms, is a reminder of the delicate yet unbreakable bond that exists between us.

Our love, much like our breath in the cold air, might seem transient, visible for only a moment before it fades away. Yet, this is the very nature of its beauty—it is ephemeral yet eternal, captured in the space between us, lingering in the chill as if to say that even the briefest moments can hold the deepest meanings.

These visible breaths, though they disappear into the winter air, leave an indelible mark on our hearts. They are reminders that in the transient nature of life, there are moments of profound significance, moments that, though they may not last forever in sight, will remain forever in our hearts.

As we navigate the path of our lives together, let us cherish these fleeting expressions of our love, knowing that their temporary visibility belies an everlasting presence. Our love is not diminished by its moments of visibility; rather, it is strengthened, its essence captured in the frosty air between us, a constant reminder of the warmth that we share, regardless of the cold that surrounds us.

Let us continue to breathe love into the air, my dearest, for each breath is a visible testament to the love that binds us—an ephemeral yet eternal promise that, regardless of how fleeting these moments may seem, our love will endure, captured forever in the memories we create and in the hearts that beat as one.

With every breath that forms in the chilly air, and with every word that we share, know that my love for you is as eternal as the cycle of seasons, as enduring as the frosty air that carries our love into eternity.

Yours, in every breath and beyond, forever yours. Charles

4. Her:

"Under the stark branches of leafless trees, we walked, our footsteps crunching in the snow, a testament to our resilience, together in solitude."

Under Stark Branches

Beneath the stark branches of trees laid bare,
We walked, our footsteps crisp in snow's embrace.
A testament to resilience we share,
Together, in solitude, we trace.

The world around us, silent and pristine,
Our path unmarked but for the steps we take.
In every crunch, a promise, a sign seen,
Of strength together, no winter can break.

These leafless guardians, stark against the sky,
Bear witness to the journey we've begun.
Through cold and chill, our love will not deny,
The warmth we carry, second to none.

Beneath these branches, our path intertwines,
A testament of love through winter's designs.

Her Love Letter:

My Beloved,

Under the stark, watchful gaze of leafless trees, our footsteps together in the snow speak volumes of the journey we've undertaken. Each crunch underfoot, a testament not just to the season's cold embrace, but to the resilience that defines us, to the solitude we share and cherish, to the path we forge together in a world that stands silent and expectant.

In this moment, with the cold air biting at our cheeks and the endless expanse of white stretching before us, I find a profound sense of peace and strength in your presence. The starkness of the landscape, with its bare branches reaching towards a grey sky, mirrors the starkness of the world we sometimes face—yet, together, we turn it into a journey of beauty, of shared solitude, of silent understanding that needs no words.

Our footsteps in the snow are fleeting, soon to be erased by the next fall, yet the resilience they symbolize, the shared determination and warmth amidst the cold, will remain indelible. We walk together, through seasons and years, through challenges and joys, each step a testament to a love that endures, that warms, that binds.

In the quiet of this winter walk, I am reminded of the many paths we have walked together and of those still to come. With each step, we reaffirm our commitment to each other, to the journey we share, to the love that guides us through every season.

Let us continue to walk together, my dearest, under the stark branches of life, finding beauty in the bareness, warmth in the cold, and a profound, resilient love in the solitude we share.

With all my love, for every step we take together,

Yours, now and always. Sognia

His Sonnet:

Solitude Together

Beneath the boughs of trees, their branches bare,
We tread through snow, our footsteps side by side.
A silent testament to the love we share,
In solitude together, we abide.

The world in winter's hold, so stark, so clear,
Yet warmth flows from our hearts, through cold it sears.
Our path marked by the steps we leave so dear,
In snow's soft bed, our resilience appears.

These trees, like sentinels in frozen pose,
Stand witness to the strength our love bestows.
Through every trial, every challenge, it grows,
Beneath winter's sky, our united glow shows.

In solitude together, our journey's song,
Beneath leafless trees, together we belong.

His Love Letter:

My Dearest,

As we walked beneath the stark branches of the leafless trees, our footsteps crunching in the freshly fallen snow, I was struck by the profound beauty of the solitude we share. Each step we took was a testament not only to the resilience that defines us but also to the unique path we have chosen to walk together, a path marked by love, companionship, and an unwavering commitment to one another.

In the silence of our winter walk, with the world around us paused and hushed under the weight of snow, I found a moment of clarity and profound gratitude for the journey we are on. The starkness of the trees, stripped of their leaves, standing resilient against the cold, mirrors our own strength in the face of challenges, our own ability to find beauty and purpose in the barest of circumstances.

Our footsteps in the snow, though temporary, are indelible in the landscape of our love. They are evidence of our presence, of our passage through this moment in time, of the resilience and warmth we carry within us, capable of withstanding the coldest of seasons.

This journey we share, marked by our footsteps under the leafless boughs, is a journey of shared solitude, of quiet strength, and of love that endures through every season. It is a journey that speaks to the essence of who we are together, a testament to the love that guides us, warms us, and gives us the courage to face the world hand in hand.

Let us continue to walk this path together, my love, finding solace in the solitude we share, strength in the resilience we embody, and an ever-deepening love in the simple act of walking side by side through the snow.

With every step we take, my heart is filled with love for you, a love that is as resilient as the bare branches overhead, as enduring as our footsteps in the snow.

Forever yours, in love and in life, Yours, always. Charles

5. Her:

"We found beauty in the ice crystals, each one unique, a mirror to our love, intricate and singular, forged in the cold yet unbowed."

Her Sonnet: Crystals of Our Love

In ice's embrace, beauty found its form,
Each crystal, unique, like our love, does shine.
Intricate, singular, against the norm,
Forged in the cold, yet unbowed, love divine.

These frozen jewels, nature's art so fine,
Reflect our bond, in myriad ways glow.
Through winter's chill, our hearts together twine,
In each unique shard, our shared love does show.

As crystals form, so does our love, in light,
Each facet, a testament, strong and clear.
Through cold and frost, our affection takes flight,
In ice, our love's resilience appears.

For in the chill, where ice crystals abound,
A mirror to our love, profound, is found.

Her Love Letter:

My Beloved,

As we walked through the winter landscape, our eyes caught the delicate beauty of ice crystals, each one a masterpiece of intricate design and singular beauty. In these frozen jewels, I saw a reflection of our love unique, complex, and incredibly beautiful, forged in the cold yet remaining unbowed and resilient.

These crystals, formed in the harshness of winter, stand as a testament to the beauty that can arise from adversity, much like our love has grown and flourished even in the face of challenges. Each crystal, with its unique pattern, reminds me of the intricate weave of our lives together, of the singular path we have forged side by side, and of the resilience that defines our bond.

In the cold, where others see harshness, we find beauty and a reflection of our own love. It is a love that, like the ice crystals, has been tested by the cold, shaped by the elements, and emerged all the more beautiful for it. Our love is intricate, filled with details and depths that only we can fully understand, and singular in its importance in our lives.

Let us continue to find beauty in the cold, my dearest, to see the reflections of our love in the world around us, and to draw strength from the resilience and uniqueness of our bond. Like the ice crystals that captivate our gaze, may our love continue to shine with a brilliance that is undimmed by the cold, a testament to the enduring and singular beauty of what we share.

With all my love, for the beauty we find together,

Yours, forever and always. Sognia

His Sonnet:

Love's Intricate Crystal

Each crystal in the cold, a work of art,
Reflects our love, so intricate and true.
In ice's grip, where most would fall apart,
Our bond, like crystals, shines a light anew.

Forged in the chill, our love stands bold and bright,
Each facet tells a tale of strength and grace.
In patterns unique, in the harshest light,
Our love's complexity finds its place.

Like ice that forms in silence, deep and still,
Our love has grown in depth, in breadth, in height.
Each crystal's form, a testament of will,
Mirrors our love, in the coldest night.

For in the frost, where each unique ice gleams,
Our love, too, shines, beyond what merely seems.

His Love Letter:

My Dearest,

In the quiet beauty of the winter's embrace, where ice crystals form with delicate precision, I find a reflection of our love. Each crystal, unique and intricate, mirrors the singular beauty of what we share complex, resilient, and undeniably beautiful, forged in the cold yet standing unbowed.

These crystals, each a testament to nature's artistry under the most challenging conditions, remind me of our journey. Just as each crystal forms its own unique pattern, so too has our love carved out its own distinct path, intricate in its details and singular in its significance. It has been shaped and tested by the cold, emerging stronger and more beautiful for the challenge.

As I marvel at the beauty of these ice crystals, I am struck by the realization that our love, too, is a masterpiece of resilience and complexity. It is a love that thrives in adversity, that finds its beauty in the depth of its uniqueness, and that stands as a testament to the enduring power of our bond.

Let us cherish the beauty found in the cold, my love, and see in it a mirror of our own love—unique, intricate, and unbreakable. Just as no two crystals are the same, so too is our love unparalleled, a singular force that withstands the chill and shines with an unmatched brilliance.

In every ice crystal, in every frosty morning, I see the beauty of what we have forged together. It is a reminder of our strength, our resilience, and the intricate beauty of our love, a love that, like the crystals, is crafted in the cold yet stands undiminished.

With all my love, for the beauty we share and the resilience we embody,

Forever yours, in love and in awe. Charles

His Reply:

"In every crystal, I saw us, complex and radiant, our love a kaleidoscope of light in the winter's grasp."

His Sonnet: Kaleidoscope of Love

In winter's grasp, where cold winds weave and twist,
Each crystal forms, a mirror to our souls.
Complex and radiant, in ice, we exist,
Our love, a kaleidoscope that enfolds.

Each facet, each angle, reflects our tale,
A myriad of moments caught in freeze.
In cold's harsh realm, our warmth does not pale,
But shines, a beacon, with the greatest ease.

Our love, like crystals, in the light, it dances,
A spectrum of joy, in winter's cold clasp.
With every turn, it shifts, it enchants us,
In love's embrace, a breathless gasp.

For in each crystal's heart, our love's displayed,
A radiant light that never will fade.

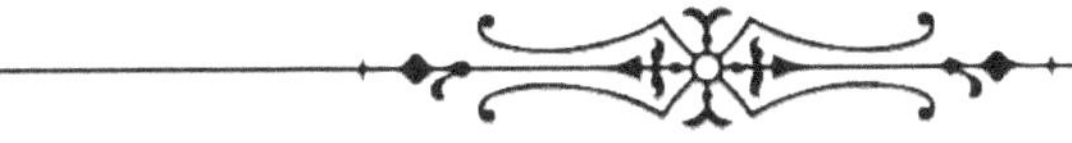

His Love Letter:

My Dearest,

As we walked through the winter landscape, each ice crystal catching the light and shimmering with a complexity that took our breath away, I saw in them a reflection of us—complex, radiant, and beautifully intricate. Each one, with its unique pattern and delicate form, was a testament to the kaleidoscopic nature of our love, a love that catches the light of our lives and reflects it in a myriad of vibrant hues.

These crystals, forged in the cold yet undiminished in their beauty, remind me of the resilience and complexity of our bond. Like them, our love has been shaped by the challenges we've faced, becoming more beautiful for the trials. In the winter's grasp, where others might see only the harshness of the cold, we find a canvas for the light of our love to shine, to dance, to illuminate the world with its warmth and brilliance.

Our love, my dearest, is indeed a kaleidoscope of light in the winter's grasp. It is ever-changing, always radiant, and endlessly fascinating. With every twist and turn of our journey together, it reveals new patterns, new beauties, a never-ending display of light and color that captivates the heart.

In every crystal that forms in the chill of winter, I see the reflections of our love complex, radiant, and unparalleled. Let us continue to shine together, my love, a kaleidoscope of light in the midst of the cold, a testament to the enduring beauty and complexity of what we share.

With all my love, for the radiant light we create together,

Yours, forever in awe of us. Charles

6. Her:

"The warmth of the fireplace became our sanctuary, flames dancing like our spirits, together against the cold outside."

Her Sonnet: Sanctuary of Warmth

In cold's vast kingdom, where frost lays its claim,
Our sanctuary found in flame's warm dance.
Together, by the fireplace, we came,
In its glow, our spirits found to prance.

The world outside may wear a frosty face,
But here, within these walls, warmth wraps us tight.
The flames, like dancers, in their fiery grace,
Reflect the fervor of our love each night.

Against the cold, our unity does stand,
A bulwark built from embers, love, and light.
Hand in hand, in warmth, together we band,
Turning the longest nights into pure delight.

For in the dance of flames, our hearts entwine,
Within this sanctuary, forever thine.

Her Love Letter:

My Dearest,

As the world outside dons its winter cloak, chilling the air and frosting the windows, we find our sanctuary by the warmth of the fireplace. Here, in the comfort of our shared space, the flames dance before us, their lively movements a mirror to the dance of our spirits, together against the cold.

In the flicker of each flame, I see the vitality of our love, the warmth that sustains us through the coldest times. This fireplace, our sanctuary, becomes more than just a source of physical warmth; it is the heart of our home, the place where our spirits come alive, where the coldness of the world outside cannot reach us.

The dance of the flames, so unpredictable and mesmerizing, reminds me of our journey together. Like these flames, our love has danced through challenges and joys, always lively, always illuminating the spaces of our lives with warmth and light. In this shared warmth, we are reminded of the strength of our bond, a bond that not only withstands the chill of the world but thrives in spite of it.

Let us cherish these moments by the fire, my love, where the warmth of the flames enfolds us and the dance of their light echoes the dance of our hearts. Here, in our sanctuary against the cold, let us hold close the warmth of our love, a warmth that comes not just from the fire before us, but from the fire within us, the fire that burns ever brighter with each passing day.

With all my love, for the warmth we share and the sanctuary we've found,

Yours, now and always, in warmth and in love. Sognia

His Sonnet:

Embers of Our Unity

Within our hearth, the flames do leap and play,
A sanctuary 'gainst the outer chill.
Together, by the fire, we find our way,
In warmth, our spirits soar, with love they fill.

The cold may press against our windowpane,
But here, inside, a different world we find.
The fire's dance, a mesmerizing chain,
Reflects the love that's ever intertwined.

These flames, like us, against the cold unite,
Their warmth a fortress, in the frosty night.
Our love, the fire that keeps the hearth alight,
In its glow, our souls together take flight.

So let the world outside grow cold and dire,
Our sanctuary lies within the fire.

His Love Letter:

My Beloved,

In the sanctuary of our home, beside the warmth of the fireplace, I find a profound sense of peace and contentment. The flames, dancing with wild and unrestrained beauty, speak to the vitality of our love, a love that warms us from within, even as the world outside succumbs to the cold embrace of winter.

This fire, our sanctuary, becomes a symbol of our union—vibrant, warm, and unwavering. It is here, in the light of the fire, that our spirits find their most lively expression, dancing together, mirroring the flames that flicker before us. The cold of the outside world fades away, leaving only the warmth that we share, a warmth that suffuses our home and our hearts.

As the flames dance, so too do our spirits, in a celebration of warmth, love, and companionship. This fireplace, the heart of our home, draws us closer, a beacon of light and warmth against the darkness and chill. It is a reminder that, together, we are more than just two souls seeking warmth; we are a united force, vibrant and alive, capable of transforming even the coldest nights into a haven of warmth and love.

Let us cherish these moments by the fire, my love, where the world outside cannot touch us, where the warmth of our love is all that matters. In this sanctuary, let us celebrate the fire that burns within us, a fire that no winter can diminish, a fire that illuminates our lives with warmth, light, and an unbreakable bond.

With all my love, for the warmth we share and the sanctuary we've created,

Yours, forever in love and warmth. Charles

His Reply:

"By the fire, I felt us meld, two flames into one, our love a fire that no winter could ever extinguish."

Melded by the Fire

By the hearth, where embers glow and breathe,
Two flames, we meld, in love's unyielding forge.
No winter's chill, nor frosty sheath,
Could dim the fire our hearts engorge.

In warmth, our spirits dance, a single blaze,
Beyond the reach of cold's encroaching hand.
Our love, a beacon through the winter's haze,
A testament to where we stand.

United by the fire's gentle kiss,
Our bond transcends the chill, the ice, the snow.
In every spark, a symbol of our bliss,
A flame that in the coldest nights will grow.

For by the fire, in love's eternal glow,
We've found a warmth that winter cannot slow.

His Love Letter:

My Dearest,

In the quiet sanctuary of our home, by the warmth of the fire, I felt an indescribable sense of unity and peace. As we sat together, the flames dancing before us, I felt our spirits meld, two flames joining in a single, radiant blaze. It was a moment of profound connection, a reminder that our love is a fire that no winter, no matter how harsh or cold, could ever extinguish.

This fire, our shared warmth, symbolizes the strength and depth of our bond. It is a fire fueled by love, by shared dreams, and by the countless moments we have spent together, each one adding to the blaze that burns brightly between us. In its warmth, I find comfort and assurance, a promise that together we can withstand any challenge, any cold that the world outside might bring.

Sitting by the fire, I realized that our love is not just a shelter against the cold—it is a vibrant, living thing, a flame that grows and intensifies with every passing moment. It is a fire that illuminates the dark, that warms the soul, and that brings a sense of home and belonging that is unparalleled.

As we move forward, hand in hand, let us carry this warmth with us, a reminder of the fire we have kindled together, a fire that no winter can dim. Let us continue to nurture this flame, to feed it with our love, our joy, and our shared experiences, so that it may ever burn bright, a beacon of love and warmth in any darkness.

With all my love, for the fire that burns between us and the warmth that it brings,

Forever yours, in love and in warmth. Charles

7. Her:

"We shared blankets and dreams, woven together, a cocoon against the winter, our aspirations as cozy as our embrace."

Her Sonnet: Cocoon of Dreams and Warmth

In winter's grasp, we found a place to dream,
Under blankets shared, our sanctuary spun.
Woven together, just like a seamless seam,
Our aspirations, warmth, and love become one.

In this cocoon, where dreams and fabric meet,
Our spirits soar on wings of shared delight.
Against the cold, a victory sweet,
In our embrace, we find our might.

Our dreams, like threads, entwined in vibrant hue,
Paint future tales on canvas broad and deep.
In warmth, our hearts find rhythms ever true,
In blankets wrapped, our promises we keep.

For in this cocoon, against winter's bite,
Our dreams, our love, in cozy warmth alight.

Her Love Letter:

My Dearest,

As the winter unfolds its chilly embrace around us, we have woven our own sanctuary, a cocoon made of blankets and dreams, where the cold cannot reach us. In the warmth of our shared space, our aspirations and our hearts find a cozy haven, as comfortable and comforting as our embrace.

This cocoon we've created, with layers of fabric and layers of hope, has become a testament to the strength and beauty of our dreams when shared. Each dream, like a thread, intertwines with another, creating a tapestry that is as rich and diverse as the love we share. In this space, our dreams do not just survive the winter; they thrive, nurtured by the warmth of our togetherness and the strength of our bond.

As we wrap ourselves in blankets, we also wrap our dreams around each other, offering warmth, support, and the promise of shared aspirations. The cold outside fades away, leaving only the heat of our dreams and the fire of our love to light the way. In our cocoon, every aspiration feels possible, every dream within reach, as long as we continue to dream them together.

Let us cherish this sanctuary we have built, my love, a place where dreams are shared as freely as the blankets that keep us warm. Let us continue to weave our aspirations into the fabric of our days, finding comfort in their shared warmth and solace in the knowledge that, together, there is no dream too distant, no aspiration too lofty.

With all my love, for the warmth of our dreams and the coziness of our embrace,

Yours, now and always, in warmth and in dreams. Sognia

His Sonnet:

Woven Dreams in Winter's Embrace

Beneath the weight of blankets, soft and deep,
Our dreams entwine, a tapestry so bright.
Against the winter's chill, our warmth we keep,
In shared cocoon, our hearts take flight.

Our aspirations, cozy as our hold,
In blankets wrapped, a future we do paint.
Together strong, together bold,
Our dreams, a sanctuary, without restraint.

The cold may howl beyond our warm abode,
But here within, our dreams in warmth are clad.
Each shared ambition, every road,
Illuminated by the love we've had.

For in this woven cocoon we've found,
Our dreams and love, in winter's silence, sound.

His Love Letter:

My Beloved,

In the quietude of winter, under the soft embrace of blankets, we have woven a sanctuary not just of warmth, but of dreams. Together, in the cozy cocoon of our shared aspirations, we find a comfort that surpasses mere physical warmth—it is the warmth of shared hopes, shared futures, and a shared life that envelops us.

As we share blankets, so too do we share our dreams, each one interlacing with the other's, creating a fabric of aspirations that is as intricate as it is strong. This cocoon we have created, a bastion against the cold, is a testament to the power of our unity, to the strength that comes from shared dreams and the warmth that arises from mutual support and love.

Within this sanctuary, every dream seems more vivid, every hope more attainable, as if the very act of sharing them imbues them with a new life, a new possibility. It is in this place, wrapped in the warmth of our embrace and the vibrancy of our dreams, that I find a profound sense of peace and purpose. Here, with you, every aspiration feels not just possible, but inevitable.

Let us hold tight to this warmth, to this shared cocoon of dreams and blankets, as we navigate the winters of our life together. May the dreams we weave today become the realities of our tomorrow and may the warmth of our embrace always be a sanctuary against the cold.

With every thread of my being, intertwined with yours, in dreams and in love,

Forever and always yours, in the warmth of our shared dreams. Charles

His Reply:

"In our shared dreams, I found a future as soft and inviting as the blankets that wrapped us, our hopes intertwined."

Future Woven Soft

In dreams we shared, a future soft was spun,
As inviting as the blankets where we lay.
Our hopes, like threads, beneath the moon and sun,
Intertwined, in love's intricate ballet.

Each aspiration, in warmth, together tied,
With every hope, our spirits further blend.
In the cocoon where our dreams reside,
We find a beginning that knows no end.

This future, woven from dreams and trust,
Holds the comfort of our shared embrace.
Against life's cold, together we must,
Find strength in love, in every shared space.

For in our dreams, a future bright we've seen,
Soft, inviting, in love's eternal sheen.

His Love Letter:

My Dearest,

In the sanctuary of our shared dreams, I have glimpsed a future as soft and inviting as the blankets under which we whisper our hopes into the night. There, in the quiet comfort of our embrace, our hopes have become intertwined, crafting a tapestry of possibilities that is as beautiful as it is boundless.

These dreams we share, each one a thread in the fabric of our future, have become the foundation upon which we build. They are soft, yet strong; ephemeral, yet eternal—a reflection of the love that wraps us as surely as the blankets do. In this shared space, our aspirations are not just dreams, but promises made in the heart, vows taken in the soul, that together, there is no future we cannot forge, no hope too distant to grasp.

Wrapped in the warmth of our cocoon, I have found not just comfort, but courage—the courage to dream bigger, to hope more fervently, and to believe in the future we are creating together. It is a future as inviting as our bed of blankets, as limitless as the night sky under which we lay, and as vibrant as the love that binds us.

Let us continue to dream, my love, for in our dreams, we find the blueprint of our future. Let us weave our hopes into every day, knowing that together, our dreams are not just possible, but inevitable. In the soft, inviting embrace of our shared aspirations, we will find our path forward, a path lit by the love we share and the dreams we dare to dream.

With all my love, for the dreams we share and the future we are weaving,

Forever intertwined, in hope and in love, Yours, always. Charles

8. Her:

"Hot cocoa with marshmallows, sweet and warm, became our potion, sipping slowly, each taste a reminder of our love's comforting presence."

Her Sonnet: Potion of Warmth and Love

In winter's chill, a potion sweet we found,
Hot cocoa with marshmallows, warmth imbued.
Each sip, a reminder, in love we're bound,
A taste of comfort, our spirits renewed.

In mugs clasped tight, where steam rises above,
Our love's essence, in each sip, does pervade.
This drink, a symbol of our tender love,
In sweetness and warmth, our affections laid.

Through frosted windows, we watch snowflakes dance,
Together, savoring our enchanted brew.
In each taste, a moment of romance,
A reminder of the love that's true.

For in this potion, sweet and warm, we find,
The comforting presence of love, entwined.

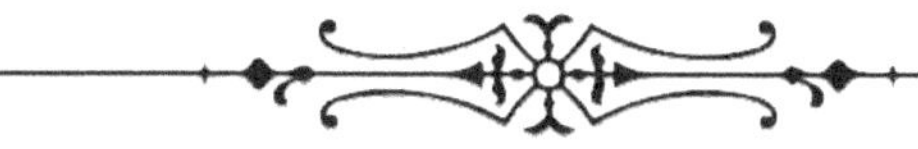

Her Love Letter:

My Dearest,

As we find solace in the warmth of our home, with winter's tapestry unfolding outside, it is in our shared moments over hot cocoa with marshmallows that I find a profound sense of comfort and connection. This simple pleasure, sweet and warm, has become more than just a drink; it has become our potion, a magical elixir that embodies the comforting presence of our love.

Each sip is a gentle reminder of the warmth that our love brings into my life, a warmth that transcends the physical and nestles deep within my soul. In the steam that rises from our mugs, I see the tangible essence of our connection—a connection that, like the heat from our cocoa, wraps me in a blanket of comfort and love.

This ritual of ours, sipping slowly, allows time to stand still, if only for a moment. It is a time for us to reconnect, to share in the simplicity of the moment, and to be reminded of the depth and sweetness of our love. With every taste, I am reminded of how our love has grown, deepened, and become as essential to me as the very air I breathe.

Let us continue to cherish these moments, my love, for they are the threads that weave the fabric of our life together. In every cup of cocoa, in every marshmallow, let us see the symbols of our love—sweet, comforting, and ever-present.

With all my love, for the sweetness and warmth you bring into my life,

Yours, always and forever, in love and in warmth. Sognia

His Sonnet:

Elixir of Our Love

In winter's heart, where cold does stake its claim,
Our potion found, in cocoa's warm embrace.
With marshmallows soft, our love the same,
Each sip a reminder of our shared space.

This elixir, sweet with warmth, does bind,
Our hearts together in its soothing spell.
In every taste, our love's comfort we find,
A story of affection, each sip does tell.

Beside the fire, with cups in hand, we sit,
The world outside may chill, but here we glow.
In cocoa's warmth, our love is lit,
A beacon against the winter's snow.

For in this drink, our love's warmth we see,
An elixir of love, for you and me.

His Love Letter:

My Dearest,

In the simple act of sharing hot cocoa with marshmallows, I have found an elixir that speaks volumes of our love. It's in these moments, sweet and warm, that the presence of our affection becomes as tangible as the mugs we hold in our hands, a comforting reminder of the love we share.

Each sip of this warm potion brings with it a sweetness that mirrors the essence of our journey together—a journey filled with moments both big and small, all of which are infused with the warmth of our love. The marshmallows, melting slowly, remind me of how our love has softened and melded over time, becoming something uniquely ours, something as comforting as the cocoa we sip.

This ritual, shared in the quiet of our sanctuary against the cold, has become a cherished pause in the rush of life, a moment to savor not just the warmth of the drink, but the warmth of us. With each sip, I am reminded of how our love has been a constant source of comfort and strength, a sweet presence that fills every corner of my life.

Let us hold onto these moments, my love, and to the reminder they bring of our love's comforting presence. For in the warmth of our cocoa, in the sweetness of our marshmallows, we find a reflection of what we share—a love that is both a comfort and a delight, a love that warms us from the inside out, even on the coldest of days.

With all my heart, for the warmth you bring into my life and the sweetness of our shared moments,

Yours, forever in love and in warmth. Charles

His Reply:

"With every sip, I tasted the sweetness of us, a concoction as potent as our love, soothing and rich."

Concoction of Us

With every sip, a sweetness found, so deep,
A concoction rich, of love's enduring brew.
In cocoa's warmth, our promises we keep,
Each taste, a testament to love so true.

This potion, potent as the bond we share,
Soothing and rich, in every drop, our tale.
In warmth, we find a refuge from despair,
A love so vast, it turns the coldest pale.

Each marshmallow, soft, dissolves like fears,
In the heat of love, no darkness nears.
With every cup, through laughter and through tears,
Our love's elixir, through the passing years.

For in this drink, our essence intertwines,
A sweet concoction of love's design.

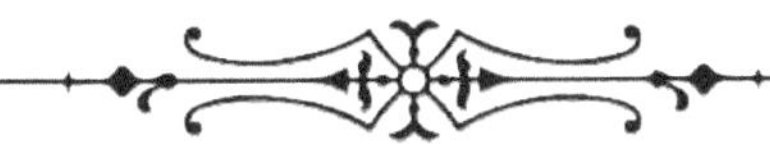

His Love Letter:

My Dearest,

In the quiet moments shared over cups of hot cocoa, with each sip, I have tasted not just the sweetness of the drink, but the sweetness of us. This concoction, rich and soothing, has become a symbol of our love—a love that is potent, comforting, and as rich as the cocoa we share.

Each taste brings with it a reminder of the depth of our connection, a blend of memories and moments that are as intricate and satisfying as the flavors of our drink. It is in these moments, my love, that I am reminded of the potency of our bond, a bond that has been a source of comfort and strength, a balm for the soul in times of need.

This cocoa, our shared elixir, is more than just a drink; it is a reflection of the richness of our journey together. With every marshmallow that melts, I am reminded of the way our love has softened the edges of life's challenges, making each moment together a little sweeter, a little warmer.

Let us continue to savor these moments, my love, each sip a celebration of the love we share. May our cups always be full, and may the sweetness of our love continue to enrich our lives, soothing and potent, through all the seasons of our life together.

With all my love, for the richness of our love and the sweetness of our moments shared,

Yours, in warmth and in love, forever. Charles

9. Her:

"The silent nights, filled with stars, whispered of infinity, our love a constant in the vastness, enduring as the night sky."

Constellations of Love

In silent nights, beneath the starry veil,
Our love whispers of infinity's breadth.
A constant in the vastness, without fail,
Enduring as the sky, with every breath.

The stars, they speak in ancient tongues of light,
Of love's enduring force through time and space.
In their eternal dance, our love takes flight,
A constellation, in the night's embrace.

This vastness overhead, the universe wide,
Mirrors the depth of love we hold inside.
Among the stars, our affections reside,
A cosmic journey, on love's tide we ride.

For in the silent nights, under star's sky,
Our love, a constant, never to die.

Her Love Letter:

My Dearest,

In the quietude of these silent nights, as we gaze upon the stars that blanket the sky, I am reminded of the infinite nature of our love. Each star, a testament to the vastness of the universe, whispers to us of eternity, of enduring truths, and of the small yet significant space we occupy within this vastness. Among these celestial bodies, our love finds its reflection a constant, unwavering presence in the infinity that surrounds us.

The night sky, with its enduring constellations, becomes a metaphor for our love. Just as the stars have guided travelers through the ages, our love guides us through the journey of life. It is a beacon in the darkness, a fixed point of light in the ever-changing tapestry of the universe.

This vast expanse above us, filled with light and mystery, mirrors the depth of the love we share. It is a love that has its own constellations, its own stories written in the light of our combined spirits. In the silence of the night, under the watchful gaze of countless stars, I feel the strength and the permanence of what we have built together.

Let us take comfort in the knowledge that our love, like the stars above, is enduring. It is a constant in a universe of change, a source of light in the darkness, and a bond that spans the reaches of time and space.

With all my love, for the infinity of us and the enduring nature of our love,

Yours, always and forever, under the starlit sky. Sognia

His Sonnet:

Love's Celestial Anchor

Beneath the dome of night, so vast, so pure,
Our love, a beacon, constant and secure.
Among the stars, it shines, forever sure,
A bond so deep, so infinite, so pure.

The silent nights, with whispers of the old,
Speak of our love, in starlight stories told.
As constellations unfold, bold and cold,
Our love's the tale that never will grow old.

In this great cosmos, vast and unexplored,
Our love's a light that's eternally adored.
Through silent nights and starry skies implored,
Our bond, a celestial chord, is stored.

For in the night's embrace, our love does fly,
A constant star, in the infinite sky.

His Love Letter:

My Dearest,

In the silence of the night, under the infinite expanse of the star-filled sky, I am reminded of the vastness of our love. Each star, a distant world of light and mystery, seems to echo the depth and constancy of the bond we share. It is in these moments, with the universe stretched out above us, that I feel the true magnitude of our love a constant in the vastness, enduring as the night sky itself.

The stars, in their silent beauty, whisper to us of eternity, of the enduring nature of love that, like them, stretches across time and space. Our love, set against the backdrop of this celestial canvas, becomes not just a personal journey, but a cosmic one, echoing the timeless dance of the universe.

This vast night sky, with its endless stars, serves as a reminder that, in the grand scheme of things, our love is a rare and precious thing—a constant light in the darkness, a fixed point in the ever-changing cosmos. It is a love that endures, not just in the here and now, but across the expanse of time, as enduring and constant as the stars themselves.

Let us cherish this love, my dearest, for it is as infinite as the night sky under which it has flourished. May we always find in each other that constant light, that enduring love, that guides us through the darkness and reminds us of the infinite possibilities that our love embodies.

With all my love, for the infinity of our bond and the enduring light of our love,

Yours, forever and always, under the stars. Charles

His Reply:

"Staring at the stars, I felt us infinite, boundless as the universe, our love a fixed star in the ever-expanding sky."

Infinite in the Starlight

Staring at the stars, our souls took flight,
Infinite, boundless, in the cosmos wide.
Our love, a fixed star, shining bright,
In the ever-expanding sky, our guide.

Amidst the galaxies, vast and deep,
Our bond, a beacon, steadfast and true.
Through cosmic winds and voids so steep,
Our love remains, in the celestial view.

In the tapestry of night, our love's a light,
A constant star, in the universe's play.
Against the dark, it stands, oh so bright,
A symbol of our love, that never will sway.

For in the starlight's infinite embrace,
Our love finds its eternal place.

His Love Letter:

My Dearest,

Under the vast expanse of the night sky, as we gazed upon the infinite array of stars, I felt a profound sense of our own boundlessness. In the quiet majesty of the universe, our love seemed to transcend the limits of time and space, becoming a fixed star in the ever-expanding sky—a beacon of light and hope in the endless night.

This moment, shared in the silent awe of the cosmos, reminded me of the eternal nature of our bond. Like the stars that have guided wanderers and dreamers through the ages, our love too is a guiding light, unwavering and steadfast, illuminating our path through life with its constant glow.

In the infinity of the night, our love finds its true expression, boundless and eternal, echoing the endless expanse of the universe. It is a love that knows no limits, that defies the constraints of the physical world, and that shines brightly against the backdrop of the cosmos.

Let us hold this moment close, my dearest, as a reminder of the vastness of our love. In the boundless beauty of the universe, our love stands as a testament to the enduring power of connection and affection—a fixed star in the ever-expanding sky, a source of light and warmth in the infinite cold.

With all my love, for the infinite journey of us,

Yours, in the boundless expanse of our love. Charles

10. Her:

"Snowflakes on your lashes, a moment captured, fleeting yet immortalized in the warmth of our laughter, melting away yet never forgotten."

Snowflakes and Memories

Upon your lashes, snowflakes gently rest,
A moment fleeting, yet forever kept.
In laughter's warmth, this memory is blessed,
Melting away, yet in our hearts adept.

These crystals, brief, in winter's soft caress,
Become the symbols of our love's light jest.
Though cold and quick to fade, their touch confess,
In transient beauty, love's endurance test.

For every flake, a whisper of our time,
A dance of nature, in our tale interwove.
With each laugh shared, our love climbs,
In memories, where fleeting moments stove.

Though snow may melt, and moments pass, it's true,
Immortalized, our love remains, in laughter's residue.

Her Love Letter:

My Dearest,

In the simple, fleeting beauty of snowflakes caught on your lashes, I found a moment so pure and ephemeral, it seemed as if time itself had paused to savor it. This moment, though it melted away as quickly as it came, has been forever etched in the warmth of our shared laughter, a memory immortalized not in ice, but in the heat of our joy.

These fleeting crystals, each one unique and momentary, are like the precious, transient moments of our life together—brief, yet capable of leaving an indelible mark on our hearts. In their melting, they remind us of the nature of time, of beauty, and of love itself: something that is at once ever-changing and eternal, melting away yet never truly gone.

This moment, with the snowflakes on your lashes and the laughter in our voices, is a testament to the enduring power of the love we share. It is a reminder that even the most fleeting moments can be captured and held in the heart, immortalized not by their permanence, but by the feelings they evoke within us.

Let us continue to cherish these fleeting moments, my love, for in them we find the essence of our journey together—a journey marked by laughter, by shared joy, and by the countless, ephemeral beauties that, like snowflakes on lashes, come into our lives to remind us of the impermanent yet unending nature of love.

With all my love, for the fleeting beauty of our moments and the eternal warmth of our laughter,

Yours, now and always, in the beauty of the fleeting and the enduring. Sognia

His Reply:

"In that fleeting touch of snow, I felt eternity, our laughter a melody that would outlast the winter."

Eternity in a Fleeting Touch

In fleeting touch of snow, eternity found,
Our laughter, a melody through winter's song.
Each flake, a note in time's profound,
In moments brief, our love grows strong.

The winter's chill, the snowflake's kiss,
Transient, yet in memory, it stays.
In every laugh, a timeless bliss,
A warmth that outlasts winter's phase.

This touch of snow, a symbol, fleeting yet deep,
Encapsulates the essence of our bond.
In laughter's melody, our love we keep,
A promise, beyond the winter, beyond.

For in that moment, brief as it may seem,
Our love, an eternal, enduring dream.

His Love Letter:

My Beloved,

In the fleeting touch of snow upon my lashes, a moment so ephemeral yet so filled with meaning, I found a profound sense of eternity. Our laughter, in that instant, became more than a simple expression of joy; it became a melody, a song that seemed destined to outlast the winter itself, echoing through time and space.

This moment, though it passed as quickly as the snowflakes melted, has imprinted itself upon my heart, a reminder of the beauty and impermanence of life, and of the enduring nature of the love we share. It was a reminder that, within the briefest touches, the shortest moments, there can exist an entire eternity, a depth of feeling and connection that transcends the physical boundaries of time.

Our laughter, in that instant, became a testament to the resilience and warmth of our bond, a warmth that defies the cold of winter, that survives beyond the fleeting and the transient. It is a melody that will continue to play, a song of love and joy and shared moments that, like the most enduring symphonies, will never truly come to an end.

Let us treasure these moments, my dearest, for they are the markers of our journey together, reminders of the laughter we've shared, the challenges we've overcome, and the endless, enduring love that binds us. In the touch of snow, in the warmth of our laughter, we find the eternal, the infinite, and the profoundly beautiful essence of our love.

With all my love, for the eternity found in every fleeting moment,

Yours, in laughter and in love, forever. Charles

11. Her:

"We ventured into the snow-covered world, adventurers in our own right, our love the compass guiding us through the white expanse."

Adventurers in Snow

Into the snow, we stepped, bold and bright,
Adventurers, with love as our guide.
The world in white, a breathtaking sight,
With love, our compass, we stride side by side.

The expanse before us, vast and unmarred,
Our footprints the only mark we leave.
In each step, our journey forward starred,
In love's embrace, we find the strength to cleave.

Through drifts deep and landscapes wide,
Our hearts warm against the cold's embrace.
In this journey, our love, our pride,
Guides us through each challenge we face.

For in this snow-covered world so vast,
Our love's the compass, true and steadfast.

Her Love Letter:

My Beloved Adventurer,

As we ventured together into the snow-covered world, stepping side by side into the vast white expanse, I felt the thrill of adventure coursing through my veins, magnified by the strength and certainty of our love. In this silent, frozen landscape, we became adventurers in our own epic tale, with love as the unwavering compass guiding our path.

Each step we took on the snow's pristine canvas marked not just our physical journey through this winter wonderland but also the journey of our hearts, bound by a love that has become our greatest adventure. The world around us, blanketed in snow, transformed into a realm of infinite possibilities, a testament to the power of our shared dreams and aspirations.

With every breath of cold air, every crunch of snow underfoot, I am reminded of the resilience and warmth of our bond. It is a love that not only guides us but also empowers us to face the unknown, to revel in the beauty of the moment, and to forge our path through the white expanse with confidence and joy.

Let us continue to venture forth, my dearest, with hearts bold and spirits high, knowing that no matter how vast the snow-covered world may seem, our love remains the truest compass, leading us to new horizons, new adventures, and a future written in the snowflakes of our shared journey.

With all my love, for the adventures we've had and those that lie ahead,

Yours, always and forever, in love and adventure. Sognia

His Reply:

"In our winter expedition, I found discovery, not of land, but of the depths of our souls, forever explorers of our boundless love."

His Sonnet: Winter's Expedition of the Soul

In winter's grasp, we ventured forth to find,
Not lands unknown, but depths within our soul.
Forever explorers, with boundless love entwined,
Our journey together, making us whole.

The snow beneath our feet, a path unmade,
Led us to discoveries profound and new.
In each other's eyes, the vastness laid,
A universe of love, endless and true.

This expedition, not of earth but heart,
Revealed the landscapes of our inner selves.
In cold's embrace, we found the warmest part,
Our love, the treasure, not found on shelves.

For in our winter wander, love's expanse,
We found our souls in every shared glance.

His Love Letter:

My Dearest,

As we embarked on our winter expedition, stepping together into the embrace of the snow-covered world, I anticipated the thrill of discovery. Yet, what I found was far more profound than any physical landscape could offer. It was not the land that we discovered, but the depths of our own souls, the boundless territories of our love.

This journey through the white expanse became an exploration of our hearts, a voyage into the essence of our bond. Each step, each shared moment in the cold, revealed new facets of our love, new strengths, and new reasons to cherish what we have. It was an expedition of the soul, where the true discovery was the depth and breadth of our connection.

In this winter wonderland, against the backdrop of untouched snow and the crispness of the air, I found a deeper understanding of us. Our love, like the landscape around us, appeared infinite, filled with possibilities and new horizons to explore. It was a reminder that we are forever explorers, not just of the physical world but of the ever-expanding universe of our love.

Let us continue this journey, my love, with the knowledge that the greatest discoveries lie not in the land under our feet but in the depths of our hearts. Our winter expedition has shown me that the most profound explorations are those we undertake together, delving into the boundless love we share.

With every step into the unknown, I find more of you, more of us, and more reasons to love you deeper. Here's to the endless expedition of our love, to the discoveries that await us, and to the boundless journey of our hearts.

Yours, forever in exploration and love, Charles

12. Her:

"The hush of winter evenings became our canvas, painting our love in shades of twilight, quiet and profound."

Twilight's Canvas

In winter's hush, our canvas spread so wide,
Painting our love in twilight's softest hues.
Quiet and profound, together we abide,
In shades of evening, our affection brews.

The silence speaks in colors deep and true,
Each stroke a testament to love's gentle might.
In dusky shades, our bond renews,
A masterpiece crafted in the fading light.

This canvas, vast, under the evening's spell,
Holds all the whispers of our hearts entwined.
In every shade, our love's story to tell,
A portrait of devotion, uniquely designed.

For in the quiet of winter evenings' glow,
Our love, in twilight shades, does ever grow.

Her Love Letter:

My Dearest,

As the world around us falls into the hushed serenity of winter evenings, I find myself captivated by the canvas it presents—a canvas where our love is painted in the tranquil, profound shades of twilight. In the quietude that envelops us, our love finds its deepest expression, its most vivid colors, painted not with brushstrokes, but with the moments we share in the gentle embrace of dusk.

These evenings have become our sanctuary, a time when the world fades away, leaving only the two of us, wrapped in the soft twilight. It is in these moments that I feel our love most acutely, a quiet force, profound and unwavering, moving within the stillness that surrounds us.

The twilight does not diminish our love; rather, it enhances its colors, adding depth and beauty that can only be appreciated in the quiet of the evening. Each shared silence, each glance exchanged under the fading light, is a hue added to the masterpiece that is our love—a masterpiece ever-changing, ever deepening, under the watchful eye of the encroaching night.

Let us treasure these twilight canvases, my love, for they are the moments when our love speaks loudest, painted in the profound shades of winter evenings. In the hush that falls with the setting sun, our love finds its voice, quiet yet powerful, painting our bond in the endless hues of dusk.

With all my love, for the beauty of our twilight moments and the depth of our shared silence,

Yours, always and forever, in the quiet and profound canvas of our love. Sognia

His Reply:

"On that canvas, I painted with you, our love the hues of dusk, deepening with each brushstroke of our hearts."

Dusk's Deepening Hues

On canvas vast, together we did paint,
Our love the hues of dusk, so rich, so bright.
With every stroke, our hearts did quaint,
The deepening shades of our affection's light.

In twilight's grasp, our colors blend and flow,
A masterpiece of love's own tender craft.
Each hue, a word, a touch we've come to know,
A memory, a smile, a look, a laugh.

This artwork of our souls, in dusky glow,
Reveals the depth of love's enduring span.
In every shade, our true emotions show,
A portrait of our bond, since it began.

For in the twilight's canvas, wide and true,
Our love's deep hues, forever in renew.

His Love Letter:

My Dearest,

As we stand together in the quiet hush of winter evenings, painting our love in the hues of dusk, I am struck by the depth and beauty of the masterpiece we create with every shared moment, every touch, every word. On this canvas, the twilight does not signify an ending but a deepening, a rich tapestry of colors that are as profound and complex as the love we share.

With you, I have learned to paint with the colors of the heart, each brushstroke a testament to the journey we've embarked upon together. Our love, like the hues of dusk, deepens with each passing moment, becoming more vibrant, more intricate, with each brushstroke of our hearts. It is a work of art that is never complete, for with each day, we add new hues, new dimensions, that make it all the more beautiful.

This canvas of twilight, where our love is painted, holds within it the promise of infinity—a promise that, no matter how the world may change, the masterpiece of our love will only grow more profound. It is a reminder that in the quiet and the calm, in the deepening shades of dusk, there is beauty, there is strength, and there is an enduring love that we continue to create together.

Let us keep painting, my love, with the hues of our hearts, on the canvas of our life together. For in the twilight of each day, in the deepening shades of dusk, I see the true colors of our love, a love that is as enduring as the night sky, as captivating as the sunset, and as hopeful as the first star that appears in the evening's glow.

With all my love, for the masterpiece we create each day,

Yours, in the deepening hues of our love, forever. Charles

13. Her:

"We celebrated the solstice, marking time, our love the constant through the cycles, brighter with each passing year."

Solstice of Our Love

Upon the solstice, time we did embrace,
Marking the cycle, our love the constant flame.
Through seasons' turn, in this celestial race,
Brighter with each year, our love became.

As days grow short, or stretch into the light,
Our bond, unyielded, stands against the tide.
In winter's chill, or summer's warmth so bright,
Together, hand in hand, we do abide.

The solstice marks not just the sun's return,
But cycles of our love, in endless churn.
With each passing year, more deeply we learn,
In love's eternal fire, we always burn.

For through the cycles, as the years do pass,
Our love, the constant, shall forever last.

Her Love Letter:

My Dearest,

As we celebrated the solstice, marking the passage of time in the eternal cycle of light and darkness, I was struck by the realization of our love as the constant through these ever-changing seasons. With each year that passes, our bond seems to grow only brighter, more resilient, mirroring the undying light that returns with greater strength with each cycle.

This moment of pause, of reflection on the turning of the world and the passage of time, serves as a reminder of the enduring nature of our love. Just as the solstice marks a point of change, a pivot in the cycle of the earth, so too does it underscore the steadfast nature of our bond, unyielding through the seasons, unwavering through the years.

In the rhythm of the earth's journey around the sun, in the cycle of light and dark, warmth and cold, I see the rhythm of our own journey together. Our love, like the light that returns each year, becomes only brighter, more profound with the passage of time. It is a beacon through the darkness, a warmth in the cold, a promise of return and renewal.

Let us take joy in the celebration of the solstice, my love, for it marks not just the passage of time, but the growth of our love through the cycles of life. With each year, with each turn of the earth, our love stands as the constant, the enduring light that guides us through the seasons, brighter with each passing year.

With all my love, for the constant light of our love through the cycles of time,

Yours, always and in all ways, through the turning of the years.
Sognia

His Reply:

"The solstice was our milestone, a marker of time and love, each year a circle completed, a spiral upwards."

Spirals of Time and Love

The solstice stands, our milestone in the sky,
A marker of both time and love's deep flow.
Each year, a circle closed, beneath its eye,
We spiral upwards, in love's warm glow.

This annual turn, a testament so clear,
To cycles of the heart, the soul's great year.
With each completion, to my heart you're near,
Our bond, a spiral, ascending without fear.

Through shortest day, or longest night's embrace,
Our love, a constant light, does never cease.
In every cycle, more beauty we trace,
In love's unending spiral, find our peace.

For solstice marks, in time's eternal dance,
Our love's progression, its endless advance.

His Love Letter:

My Dearest,

As we celebrate the solstice, marking the passage of time with a reverence that mirrors the cycles of the earth itself, I find myself reflecting on the beautiful spiral of our love. This annual milestone, far from merely signifying another year passed, represents a circle completed in the ongoing journey of our hearts—a spiral that climbs ever upwards, reaching towards new heights with each turn.

This solstice, like those before it, serves as a poignant reminder of our journey together, of the time marked not in hours and days, but in moments shared, challenges faced, and joys celebrated. It is a testament to the enduring nature of our love, a love that grows more profound, more radiant with each passing year.

In the cyclical nature of the solstice, in the dance of light and darkness, warmth and cold, I see the dance of our own lives, a dance marked by the constant presence of our love. With each year, with each cycle, our love completes another circle, adding to the spiral that moves ever upwards, guided by the light of our shared dreams and aspirations.

Let us cherish the solstice, my love, as a marker of time and love, a celebration of the cycles we've completed and the spirals we've ascended. Each year, with each circle closed, we are reminded of the journey we've undertaken together, a journey that continues to spiral upwards, filled with endless possibilities and boundless love.

With all my heart, for the milestones we've marked and the spirals we've climbed,

Yours, in love's endless ascent, through the cycles of time. Charles

14. Her:

"Ice skating on a frozen pond, our laughter breaking the silence, a dance of joy on the ice, carefree in the cold."

Dance on Ice

Upon a frozen pond we twirled, a pair,
Our laughter slicing through the silent air.
A dance of joy upon the ice so fair,
In winter's grip, we found a moment rare.

Our skates carved paths where none had been before,
A tapestry of lines in cold's embrace.
With every turn, our spirits did soar,
Carefree we moved, in love's own graceful chase.

The chill around, but warmth within our hearts,
A contrast to the ice beneath our feet.
In every laugh, a melody imparts,
A song of joy, in winter's cold, complete.

For on that pond, beneath the winter's dome,
We danced a dance that felt like coming home.

Her Love Letter:

My Dearest Love,

As we glided together across the frozen pond, our laughter mingling with the crisp winter air, I was struck by the pure joy of the moment. Ice skating with you, in this beautiful, silent world, felt like a dance of joy, a celebration of life and love, unencumbered by the cold that surrounded us.

Each stroke of our skates on the ice, each burst of laughter that broke the silence, was a testament to the carefree happiness we share. In these moments, with you, I am reminded of the simple pleasures that life offers us, the moments of unbridled joy that come from being with the one you love, doing something as simple yet as exhilarating as skating on a frozen pond.

The coldness of the air, the hardness of the ice, none of it mattered as long as we were together, dancing our dance of joy, carefree in the embrace of winter. It was as if the world had paused, giving us this moment to revel in our happiness, to celebrate our love in the most joyful of dances.

Let us cherish these moments, my love, for they are the essence of our journey together. In the laughter, in the dance, in the carefree joy we find with each other, we find the true warmth that sustains us through the cold, the love that keeps us dancing through life, together and joyous.

With all my love, for the dances we've shared and those yet to come,

Yours, always and forever, in joy and in love. Sognia

His Reply:

"Skating with you, I found freedom, our dance a defiance of winter, a celebration of warmth in the cold."

Freedom on Ice

With you, upon the ice, I found my flight,
A dance that dared the winter's chill defy.
In glides and turns, our hearts took to the night,
A celebration, 'neath the cold sky.

This frozen pond, our stage for freedom's play,
Where laughter echoes, warmth against the frost.
Together, in defiance, we convey,
That in this cold, not all is lost.

Our dance, a testament to warmth within,
A bond that winter's touch could never freeze.
In every step, together we begin,
To find our joy, our love, our ease.

For skating with you, through the cold we soared,
A freedom found, in love's warm chord.

His Love Letter:

My Dearest,

As we took to the ice, hand in hand, skating together through the silent, frozen world, I discovered a sense of freedom that I had never known before. It was as if, with each glide and turn across the pond, we were not just defying the grip of winter, but celebrating the warmth that exists between us, a warmth that the cold could not touch.

This dance of ours on the ice, amidst the chill of the air and the stark beauty of the winter landscape, became a declaration of our joy, our love, and our resilience. In the freedom of our movements, in the laughter that filled the air, I found the essence of our connection—a bond that thrives in defiance of the cold, that finds celebration in the very heart of winter.

The coldness of the world around us faded into insignificance as we danced our defiant dance, reveling in the warmth of our togetherness. It was a reminder that, even in the coldest of times, the warmth we share is our greatest strength, our most profound celebration, a source of joy and freedom that nothing can diminish.

Let us carry this sense of freedom with us, my love, as we journey through the seasons of life. For in the dance we share, in the defiance of the cold and the celebration of our warmth, we find not just joy, but a deeper understanding of the love that binds us, a love that is as free and as boundless as our spirits on the ice.

With all my heart, for the freedom and warmth we share,

Yours, in love and in celebration, always. Charles

15. Her:

"We gathered around the table for winter feasts, our love the unspoken guest, filling the room with warmth and gratitude."

Feast of Love

Around the table, in winter's deep embrace,
We gathered close, our spirits bright and keen.
Our love, the guest unspoken in this place,
Filling the room with warmth, unseen but seen.

Each dish, a testament to care and thought,
A bounty spread, from heart and hearth derived.
In every bite, a story wrought,
Of love and gratitude, fully inscribed.

The laughter shared, the stories told,
Beneath the glow of candle's tender light.
In these feasts, our love unfolds,
A celebration, in the cold night.

For around this table, love's warmth we greet,
In every feast, our hearts' joy complete.

Her Love Letter:

My Dearest,

As the cold of winter wraps around us, it is at our table, surrounded by the bounty of winter feasts, that I am most acutely aware of the warmth and richness of our love. It becomes the unspoken guest at every gathering, a presence felt by all, enveloping the room in an aura of warmth and gratitude that surpasses the glow of candles and the heat of the meal before us.

Each dish prepared and shared is a manifestation of the care we hold for one another, a tangible representation of love that nourishes far more than just our bodies. It is in these moments, as we share food, laughter, and stories, that I am reminded of the abundance that our love brings into our lives, an abundance that fills not just our table but our hearts and our home.

This love, so often unspoken yet ever-present, is what transforms a simple meal into a feast, a gathering into a celebration. It is the warmth that combats the cold outside, the gratitude that turns thoughts of scarcity into acknowledgments of plenty. Our gatherings around the table become sacred rituals, celebrations of the love that sustains us, the joy that we share, and the community we build together.

Let us continue to welcome this unspoken guest, my love, to our table and into our lives, knowing that with each meal shared, with every story told and laugh exchanged, our love only grows deeper, richer, and more profound. It is this love that makes every winter feast a feast of the heart, a celebration of the warmth and gratitude that we share.

With all my love, for the feasts we share and the love that fills our home,

Yours, now and always, in warmth and in gratitude. Sognia

His Reply:

"At the table, our love was the feast, nourishing and full, a banquet of moments shared in the heart of winter."

Banquet of Love

At our table, love itself was the feast,
Nourishing, full, in winter's cold embrace.
A banquet laid of moments not the least,
In every shared smile, a warmth we trace.

Our hearts, the plates from which we dine,
On laughter, stories, and tender care combined.
Each glance, a sip of the finest wine,
In love's banquet, our souls entwined.

The cold outside could never chill,
The warmth within, our love does fill.
For at our table, time stands still,
A celebration of love's own will.

In the heart of winter, our feast of love,
A banquet blessed from stars above.

His Love Letter:

My Beloved,

In the heart of winter, around our table, I have come to realize that our love is the true feast, a banquet not of dishes and delicacies, but of moments shared and memories made. It is nourishing, full, and richer than any meal could ever be, a testament to the abundance that we have created together in our shared life.

Each laugh, each story, each look shared across the table becomes a course in this banquet of love, serving to strengthen the bond between us and to fill our hearts with joy. It is in these gatherings, in the heart of winter, that I am most deeply grateful for the love we share, a love that sustains us, nourishes us, and brings warmth to even the coldest of days.

This banquet of love, laid out in the simple moments of togetherness, reminds me that the true measure of our wealth lies not in the material but in the depth and quality of our connections. Our love, shared freely and fully, is the most exquisite of feasts, one that satisfies the soul and fills the heart to overflowing.

As we continue to gather around the table, through winters yet to come, let us remember that it is our love that is the feast, our shared moments the dishes from which we draw sustenance and strength. May we always find nourishment in our love, fullness in our togetherness, and warmth in the heart of winter.

With all my love, for the banquet of moments we share,

Yours, in love and gratitude, forevermore. Charles

16. Her:

"The winter's moon watched over us, a silent guardian, illuminating our path, its glow a reminder of the enduring light of our love."

Guardian Moon

Beneath the winter's moon, we found our way,
A silent guardian in the sky so high.
Its glow, a beacon, night turned almost day,
Illuminating paths where our love lies.

This celestial watcher, cold and bright,
Bears witness to the constancy of heart.
In its soft glow, our love finds its light,
A reminder that we're never far apart.

Through darkest nights and coldest winter's breath,
The moon above, a steadfast friend, does shine.
In its enduring light, no hint of death,
But life, and love, that's evermore divine.

For in the moon's glow, softly we're assured,
Our love's enduring light is ever-preserved.

Her Love Letter:

My Dearest,

In the quiet of the winter nights, as we walk side by side under the watchful gaze of the moon, I am comforted by its presence— a silent guardian that illuminates our path with its gentle glow. It reminds me of the enduring light of our love, a constant force that guides us through the darkness, warming our hearts with its unwavering brightness.

The moon, with its serene light, seems to watch over us, blessing our journey with its luminance. In its glow, every shadow is softened, every path cleared, mirroring the way our love illuminates our lives. It is a reminder, in the stillness of the night, of the enduring nature of what we share, a love that, like the moon's light, remains constant and true, no matter the darkness that surrounds us.

As we walk beneath its glow, hand in hand, I am struck by the beauty of its silent vigil, a celestial guardian that mirrors the protective warmth of our love. It is a beacon in the night, a symbol of hope and continuity, reminding us that even in the coldest, darkest times, there is light, there is warmth, and there is love.

Let us cherish the glow of the winter's moon, my love, for in its light, we see the reflection of our own enduring bond. May we always find our way by its luminescence, guided by the light of our love, comforted by the knowledge that, no matter where we go, we are watched over, protected, and loved.

With all my love, under the guardian glow of the moon,

Yours, always and in all ways, bathed in the enduring light of our love. Sognia

His Reply:

"Beneath the winter moon, I felt watched over, our path illuminated by its gentle glow, our love safeguarded."

His Sonnet: Beneath the Winter Moon

Beneath the watchful eye of winter's moon,
Our path aglow with its soft, silvered light.
Felt watched over, as if the stars did swoon,
Our love safeguarded through the coldest night.

This lunar guardian, silent in its watch,
Illuminates the way our hearts have trod.
In its presence, our fears and doubts are botched,
Guided by the glow, on love's path, we plod.

The moon, a beacon in the winter's chill,
Its gentle glow, a shield against the dark.
In its light, our love finds the will
To flourish, even when the world seems stark.

Beneath its glow, our journey feels endowed,
Our love, under the moon's watch, proudly avowed.

His Love Letter:

My Dearest,

As we walked together beneath the winter moon, its gentle glow casting a silvered path before us, I was struck by a profound sense of being watched over, protected by its luminous presence. This guardian light, so soft and yet so powerful, seemed to safeguard our love, illuminating our way through the darkness, ensuring that no shadow could diminish the warmth between us.

In the serene light of the moon, I felt our love was not just witnessed but cherished by the universe itself. This celestial body, hanging silent and majestic in the sky, became for me a symbol of the enduring nature of our bond, a reminder that, no matter the obstacles, our path together is illuminated by a light that never fades.

This sense of safeguarded love, of a path brightly lit by the moon's gentle glow, fills me with a deep gratitude and a renewed sense of commitment. It reassures me that, no matter the darkness that might surround us, the light of our love will always find a way to shine through, guided and protected by the watchful eyes of the heavens.

Let us always remember this feeling of being watched over, my love, as we continue our journey together. Beneath the winter moon, in its protective glow, our love is not just safeguarded but celebrated, a bright flame burning steadily in the heart of the night.

With all my love, for the illuminated path we walk together,

Yours, in the gentle glow of our safeguarded love. Charles

17. Her:

"We found solace in the quietude of winter, a peace within the storm, our love a shelter from the swirling snow."

Shelter in the Storm

In winter's hush, solace we did find,
A peace within the tumult of the storm.
Our love, a shelter, steadfast and kind,
Against the snow's swirl, a protective form.

The world outside may rage with icy gusts,
But in our hearts, a calm does firmly dwell.
Through flurries fierce, in love, we place our trusts,
Within this haven, our spirits swell.

As snowflakes dance in frenzied, wild display,
Within our grasp, tranquility takes hold.
Our love, the flame that keeps the cold at bay,
A refuge warm, against the outside cold.

For in the quietude of winter's embrace,
Our love, a shelter, finds its perfect place.

Her Love Letter:

My Beloved,

In the serene quietude of winter, as the world outside succumbs to the silence of the snow, I have found an unparalleled solace in your love. It is a peace that feels profound, a calm within the storm, a shelter that holds firm against the swirling snow and the icy winds that howl at our door.

This love of ours, it stands as a bastion against the winter's chill, a warm embrace that protects and comforts in the midst of nature's fury. Within the sanctuary of our love, the storm outside fades to a mere whisper, its fierceness tempered by the strength of our bond.

In the tranquility of these moments, with the world held at bay, I am reminded of the power of our love. It is a force that not only shelters but nurtures, transforming the coldness of winter into a season of warmth and introspection. In your love, I find a haven, a quiet place where the storm cannot reach, where the snow is but a backdrop to the enduring warmth that burns between us.

Let us cherish this peace, my dearest, for it is in these moments of quietude that our love shines the brightest. As winter unfolds around us, let us take comfort in the shelter we provide for each other, a refuge from the storm, a sanctuary of warmth in the cold. Our love is the peace within the storm, a testament to the strength and depth of the bond we share.

With all my love, for the shelter of your love and the peace it brings,

Yours, always and in all ways, in the quietude of winter. Sognia

His Reply:

"In that quietude, I found my peace, in the eye of the storm, with you, our love the sanctuary from winter's fury."

Sanctuary in the Storm

In winter's quietude, my peace was found,
Within the storm's fierce eye, there stood a calm.
With you, my heart's true sanctuary bound,
Our love, a balm against the winter's harm.

Around us raged the tempest's icy blast,
Yet in your arms, I found a warmth so true.
A haven from the fury, holding fast,
Our love, the shelter that my spirit knew.

This love of ours, more than mere refuge,
A fortress 'gainst the season's chill embrace.
Within its walls, our hearts did merge and fuse,
In the storm's eye, we found our sacred space.

For in the quietude with you, my dear,
The winter's fury we no longer fear.

His Love Letter:

My Dearest,

In the enveloping silence of the winter, as the world around us succumbed to the might of the storm, I found an unparalleled peace in the sanctuary of our love. It was in this quietude, in the very eye of the storm, that the true depth of our bond was revealed to me, a haven untouched by the fury of winter's assault.

With you, amidst the swirling snow and the howling winds, I found a warmth and a safety that the coldest winter could not breach. Our love became my sanctuary, a sacred space where the storm's rage could not reach, where the chill of the season was banished by the heat of our affection.

This peace that I found with you, in the heart of the storm, is a testament to the strength of our love. It is a sanctuary not built of walls and roofs, but of trust, understanding, and the shared warmth of two hearts in perfect union. In your presence, the winter's fury fades into insignificance, its power nullified by the sanctuary of our love.

Let us hold fast to this quietude, my love, to the peace we find in each other, no matter the storms that rage around us. For in the sanctuary of our love, we have found a fortress against the winter, a warm haven where our souls can rest and our spirits can soar, untouched by the fury of the outside world.

With all my love, for the peace and sanctuary you provide,

Yours, in the eye of the storm, forever and always. Charles

18. Her:

"As the year waned, we looked forward to renewal, our love undimmed by the cold, a flame ready to burst forth with the spring."

Love's Renewal

As year wanes and cold winds keenly blow,
We stand firm, our love's flame undimmed,
A beacon against winter's frosty show,
In darkness, our light has never skimmed.

Awaiting spring, our hearts in patience bide,
Our love, a seed beneath the snow, lies quiet,
Ready to burst forth, with time as guide,
In renewal's dance, our flame a riot.

Through cold's long reign, our warmth sustains,
A promise held in love's enduring spark.
For when the ice thaws and green regains,
Our love will bloom, a fire against the dark.

As the year turns, in cold's deep embrace,
Our love awaits spring's renewing grace.

Her Love Letter:

My Beloved,

As the year slowly wanes and the cold wraps its fingers around the world, I find a deep comfort in the unwavering warmth of our love. Despite the chill that pervades, our love remains a flame undimmed, burning with a brightness that defies the darkness of winter, a promise of renewal that lies in wait.

In these moments, as we look forward to the rebirth of spring, I am reminded of the enduring nature of our bond. Our love, much like the earth beneath the snow, quietly harbors the promise of new growth, of vibrant blooms that will burst forth when the warmth returns. It is a love ready to embrace the renewal that spring brings, to flourish anew in the light of longer days.

This season of waiting, of anticipation, only deepens the love we share, for it is filled with the promise of what is yet to come. Our love, undimmed by the cold, stands as a testament to the cycles of life, a cycle of dying and rebirth, of endings and new beginnings. It is a flame that not only survives the winter but is made all the more ready to burst forth with the spring.

Let us cherish this time of quiet anticipation, my love, for it is the precursor to a season of growth and renewal. As the year wanes, let us look forward to the warmth and vibrancy of spring, secure in the knowledge that our love, like the earth itself, is ready to embrace the renewal that lies just beyond the cold.

With all my love, for the promise of renewal and the undimmed flame of our love,

Yours, in anticipation of spring's warmth and the renewal of our love. Sognia

His Reply:

"In the waning year, I saw not an end but a promise, our love the ember from which the new fire of spring would ignite."

Ember of Promise

In waning year, where others see the close,
I saw a promise, in our love, an ember.
Not an end, but start, from which there grows
A new fire of spring, bright and tender.

This ember, our love, in cold's deep hold,
Awaits the touch of spring's renewing breath.
From it, a blaze of passion, bold,
Will rise, defying winter's chill and death.

Our love, the seed from which new life springs,
Through darkest nights, its warmth endures, it clings.
To the promise of what the future brings,
In love's eternal fire, our hearts take wings.

So, in the year's decline, we find not fright,
But hope in love's enduring, burning light.

His Love Letter:

My Dearest,

As the year wanes and the landscape of our world is drawn into the quietude of winter, I find within me not a sense of ending, but a profound promise—a promise embodied by the ember of our love, glowing with the potential for new beginnings, for renewal and growth.

This ember, the very essence of our love, harbors the promise of the new fire of spring, ready to ignite with the first breath of warmth, to burst forth into a blaze that lights up our world with its vibrancy and heat. It is a reminder that in every ending there lies the seed of a new beginning, a cycle of life and love that is eternal and unending.

In the cold and the darkness, it is our love that remains the constant, the ember from which the future is kindled. It is a source of warmth and light, a beacon that guides us through the shortest days and the longest nights, always with the promise of renewal, of a spring that will come again, bringing with it the flourishing of all that we have nurtured together.

Let us hold fast to this promise, my love, as we move through the winter. Let us cherish the ember of our love, knowing that from it will come the new fire of spring, a testament to the enduring strength and vitality of our bond. In the heart of winter, let us find comfort and joy in the knowledge that our love is the promise of spring, the promise of new beginnings and endless renewal.

With all my love, for the ember that is our promise and the fire that is our future,

Yours, in the promise of renewal and the warmth of our enduring love. Charles

19. Her:

"We traced patterns in the frost, a temporary art, our love the artist, creating beauty in the transient, the fleeting made eternal."

Artistry in Frost

In frost's embrace, our fingers traced,
A canvas wide, where chill winds brushed.
Our love, the artist, finely laced,
In transient beauty, cheeks flushed.

Each pattern in the frost, a fleeting mark,
Yet in our hearts, these designs eternal stay.
Our love, a light within the stark,
Creating beauty in the brief display.

The temporary art, in cold air drawn,
Speaks of love's power to seize the day.
In fleeting moments, before they're gone,
Our love inscribes its presence, come what may.

For in the frost, our transient art,
We find the eternal within our heart.

Her Love Letter:

My Dearest,

As we ventured out into the crisp, cold air, our breaths visible in the morning light, we found a canvas awaiting us in the frost that adorned every surface. Together, with our love as the artist, we traced patterns in the frost, creating a temporary art that spoke of the beauty and impermanence of the moment.

This art, so fleeting and yet so full of meaning, is a testament to the creativity and joy that our love brings into every aspect of life. Each pattern, each line drawn in the frost, was a reflection of the beauty we create together, of the transient made eternal through the strength and depth of our bond.

In these moments, as we watched our breaths mingle with the cold air and our fingers leave their mark upon the frost, I was reminded of the incredible power of our love to find beauty in the fleeting, to create moments of wonder and awe in the most ordinary of settings. It is a reminder that, though our art may disappear with the morning sun, the love that inspired it remains, a constant force that continues to shape our world in ways both seen and unseen.

Let us continue to create, my love, to leave our mark upon the world in ways both big and small. For in the artistry of our love, we find a beauty that endures, transcending the transient and leaving a lasting imprint upon our hearts.

With all my love, for the beauty we create and the transient moments we make eternal,

Yours, always and in all ways, in love and artistry. Sognia

His Reply:

"With each pattern, I saw our impermanence and our infinity, our love the masterwork in the frost, ephemeral yet everlasting."

Impermanence and Infinity

With each pattern traced in morning's frost,
Impermanence and infinity were found.
Our love, the masterwork, at no cost,
Ephemeral in form, yet unbound.

In transient crystals, beauty brief,
We saw our love's reflection, pure and true.
A moment's art, in its life, so chief,
Yet in our hearts, its essence ever new.

The frost may melt beneath the sun's keen gaze,
Our patterns lost to warmth's relentless tide.
But in this cycle, our love displays,
Eternal strength, where true essences reside.

For in the frost, our love's paradox we see,
Ephemeral yet everlasting, free.

His Love Letter:

My Dearest,

As we traced patterns in the frost, our fingers weaving together a tapestry of the temporary and the eternal, I was struck by the profound duality of our existence. In each pattern, I saw not just the fleeting beauty of the moment, but a reflection of the impermanence and infinity that define our love—a love that, like our art in the frost, is ephemeral in its expression yet everlasting in its impact.

This dance of creation and dissolution, of patterns emerging and then fading away under the morning sun, speaks to the very essence of our love. It is a masterwork in the frost, a masterpiece that captures the heart of what it means to love and be loved—knowing that while the expressions of our affection may be temporary, the love that inspires them is eternal, transcending the bounds of time and space.

In the frost, I saw the beauty of our impermanence, the preciousness of each moment we share, knowing it will not last. And yet, within this impermanence, I found a deeper truth—the infinity of our love, a force that, though it may change form, will never cease to exist, continuing to inspire, to warm, and to guide us, long after the frost has melted.

Let us cherish this duality, my love, embracing the ephemeral beauty of the moment while holding fast to the everlasting essence of our love. For in the transient art we create, in the patterns we trace in the frost, we find the enduring masterwork of our hearts, a love that is both ephemeral and eternal, a paradox that binds us together, forever.

With all my love, for the impermanence and infinity of us,

Yours, in the ephemeral and the everlasting. Charles

20. Her:

"I loved you like that, through the silent watch of winter, our love a testament to warmth, to growth, and to the promise of rebirth."

Her Final Sonnet:

Testament of Seasons

I loved you through the silent watch of snow,
Our love, a testament to warmth within.
Through winter's grasp, our steadfast hearts did grow,
Against the cold, our warmth did surely win.

As silent sentinels, the trees stood bare,
Yet in their quiet, promised life anew.
So our love, in the cold air, did declare,
A promise of rebirth, of starting true.

Through frost and chill, our love did not just survive,
But flourished, bloomed, against the odds did thrive.
A testament to what it means to strive,
Together, ensuring our love stays alive.

For in the silent watch of winter's night,
Our love stood firm, a beacon of warm light.

Her Final Love Letter:

My Dearest,

As we find ourselves nearing the end of this season, both in the cycle of the year and in the cycle of our own story, I am moved to reflect on the journey we have shared. I loved you like that, through the silent watch of winter, with a love that has been a testament to warmth in the midst of cold, to growth amidst the stillness, and to the undying promise of rebirth.

In the quiet of the winter, in the watchful presence of the bare trees and the crisp air, our love has proven itself to be a force of nature, as inevitable as the spring that follows the cold. It is a love that has not only endured but has grown deeper, more resilient, and more beautiful with each passing day.

This season of winter, with its silent nights and frosty mornings, has been but a backdrop to the warmth we have nurtured within our hearts—a warmth that has sustained us, that has been our beacon through the darkest nights and the coldest days. It is this warmth, this love, that stands as a testament to our journey together, a journey marked by the promise of continual renewal, of new beginnings, and of endless growth.

As we stand on the threshold of spring, looking forward to the rebirth that awaits us, let us carry forward the lessons of this winter. Let us remember that our love, like the seasons, is ever-changing, ever-growing, and ever-renewing. It is a love that has carried us through the silent watch of winter and will continue to guide us through all the seasons of our life together.

With all my love, for the warmth we've shared, the growth we've cherished, and the promise of rebirth that lies ahead,

Yours, forever and always, in love and in gratitude, at the end of winter and the beginning of all that comes next. Sognia

His Reply:

"And I loved you like that, as a vow against the cold, our love the spring waiting beneath the snow, ready to bloom anew.

His Final Sonnet:

Vow Against the Cold

And I loved you, as winter's vow so bold,
Against the cold, our hearts did not despair.
Our love, the spring beneath the frost and cold,
Awaiting warmth, to bloom anew, so fair.

This love, a promise made in winter's chill,
To thrive, to grow, as seasons shift and sway.
Beneath the snow, a warmth that cannot still,
A force that waits for spring's return, to play.

Through silent nights and frosty mornings clear,
Our love endured, a seed beneath the freeze.
A testament to all that we hold dear,
In love's vow, we find our hearts' ease.

For in the vow against the cold, we find,
Our love, the spring, in winter's grasp, entwined.

His Final Love Letter:

My Dearest,

As we stood together in the embrace of winter, our love became a vow against the cold a promise that, beneath the blanket of snow, the seeds of our spring lay waiting, ready to burst forth into bloom with the first whisper of warmth. This vow, this love, has been the silent undercurrent of our journey through the winter, a steadfast belief in the renewal and growth that await us on the other side of the cold.

Our love, like the spring waiting beneath the snow, has not been deterred by the frost, by the chill that sought to envelop us. Instead, it has grown stronger, more resilient, drawing from the cold itself a promise of rebirth, of renewal, of a beauty yet to be revealed. It is a love that speaks of the infinite cycle of life, of the enduring dance between the seasons, and of the inevitable return of warmth and light.

As we prepare to bid farewell to winter, to welcome the thaw and the blossoming of all that has been hidden beneath the snow, I am filled with a deep gratitude for the love that has carried us through. It is a love that has proven itself to be as inexorable as the seasons, as hopeful as the first buds of spring, and as vibrant as the life that pulses beneath the frozen earth, waiting for its moment to emerge.

Let us move forward, my love, with the knowledge that our love is the spring beneath the snow, ready to bloom anew. It is a vow against the cold, a promise of warmth, of growth, and of the endless beauty that lies in wait, ready to unfold in the light of our shared journey.

With all my love, for the vow we've made and the spring that awaits,

Yours, in the promise of renewal and the warmth of our enduring love. Charles

In the quietude of winter, where each snowflake whispers tales of resilience, and the frost paints portraits of serene beauty on windowpanes, we find a gentle farewell to the four seasons of a love story that has traversed the spectrum of life's offerings. From the hopeful blossoms of spring, through the warm, vibrant days of summer, into the rich, reflective embrace of autumn, and finally resting in the introspective calm of winter, this journey has been a testament to the enduring power of love.

Spring brought the promise of new beginnings, a canvas fresh and vibrant, where love took root in the fertile ground of young hearts. It was a time of discovery, of firsts, where every touch, every glance, was a seed planted with the promise of growth.

Summer saw the flourishing of this love under a sunlit sky, a period of warmth, of joy unfettered, where love basked in the light of day, bold and unafraid. The world was alive, and so was the love that thrived within it, a testament to the abundance that life offers when hearts are open and free.

Autumn brought the richness of maturity, a deepening of colors, of emotions, as the love story continued to unfold. It was a season of reflection, of gratitude for the journey thus far, and of preparation for the times to come. Love, like the leaves, turned deeper shades, enriched by the experiences shared and the memories made.

And then came Winter, with its quiet introspection, its challenges and serene beauty, paralleling the depth and resilience of love amidst the backdrop of life's quieter moments. It was a time of huddling close, of sharing warmth, of lighting the dark with the flame of enduring affection. Winter was a testament to the strength found in stillness, in the shared silence, in the beauty of a love that has weathered all seasons.

As we bid farewell to these seasons of life and love, let us carry forward the lessons learned with each passing year. May the hope of spring, the warmth of summer, the richness of autumn, and the serene introspection of winter remain with us, guiding our steps like the ever-present cycle of the seasons. In the quiet landscape of winter, we find not an end, but a promise—a promise of renewal, of continued growth, and of love's enduring light, shining ever bright, ever constant, through the seasons of life.

Farewell to the seasons, to the chapters of a story that will continue to inspire, long after the last snow has melted, leaving behind the eternal spring of love reborn, ever vibrant, evergreen.

Her Final Sonnet:

Sum of All Seasons

In unison we stand, at journey's end,
Reflecting on the seasons we've traversed.
Through spring's bright dawn, to summer's light, we've wend,
In autumn's glow, and winter's chill conversed.

We've touched the lives like leaves in breezy swirl,
Climbed mountains high, where eagles dare to soar.
Through storms we've sailed, our love the flag unfurl,
A beacon steadfast on life's rugged shore.

Together we have built, with hands entwined,
A legacy of love, of joy, of pain.
In every trial, a silver lining find,
In every loss, together found our gain.

At day's end, as we marvel, side by side,
Our love, the sum of all, our constant guide.

Her Final Love Letter:

My Beloved Companion,

As we stand together, hand in hand, at the end of our journey, looking back on the tapestry of seasons we've woven together, I am overwhelmed with a sense of awe and gratitude. From the fresh blossoms of our spring, through the sun-drenched days of our summer, into the rich harvest of our autumn, and finally, into the quiet reflection of our winter, we have lived a life of remarkable depth, beauty, and love.

We have touched lives, leaving imprints of kindness and warmth that will outlast our footsteps. We climbed mountains, facing challenges that tested our resolve and strengthened our bond. We weathered storms, finding shelter in each other, our love a beacon that guided us through the darkest nights.

As we look back, marveling at the sum of it all, I am struck by the beauty of what we have built together. Our love, a remarkable journey that has encapsulated the essence of all four seasons, stands as a testament to the enduring power of a life well-lived and shared.

In the twilight of our days, as we reflect on the sum of our seasons, I find myself cherishing not just the moments of triumph and joy, but every moment we've shared. For it is in the sum of these moments, both big and small, that our life together finds its true meaning and beauty.

Thank you, my dearest, for being my partner through every season, for sharing this journey with me, for the love, the laughter, the tears, and the memories that we have created together. As we stand in unison, looking back and marveling at our journey, I am filled with a profound sense of peace and fulfillment, knowing that we are, indeed, the sum of it all.

With all my love, now and forever,

Yours, in reflection, gratitude, and everlasting love. Sognia

His Final Sonnet:

Reflections at Journey's End

Side by side, as seasons round did turn,
We crafted a life from love, bold and vast.
Each challenge faced, a chance to live, to learn,
In love's warm glow, each storm we did outlast.

From spring's first kiss to winter's gentle hush,
Our journey's path, with memories, is paved.
Through every high and low, our hearts did rush,
In every moment, love's beauty we've craved.

Now, as we stand, the sum of all we've been,
Our legacy in hearts we've touched, we see.
A life of love, of sights and wonders seen,
Together, always was meant to be.

At journey's end, we look back, understand,
Our love, the sum, more beautiful, more grand.

His Final Love Letter:

My Dearest Partner in Life,

As we stand together, witnessing the dusk of our journey, I am enveloped by a profound sense of completeness. Reflecting on the seasons of our life well-lived, I see not just the passage of time but the remarkable tapestry we've woven together, a masterpiece of love, resilience, and shared dreams.

From the hopeful springs of our youth, through the bountiful summers of our love's maturity, into the reflective autumns of our contentment, and now, in the peaceful winter of our days, we have lived fully, loved deeply, and left a mark on the world and on each other's hearts.

We have built a life that is a testament to the enduring strength of love, climbing mountains of challenges, weathering the storms of life, and marveling at the beauty of our shared journey. Each season brought its own gifts, its own lessons, and together, we have gathered them all, cherishing the warmth, the growth, and the promise of rebirth inherent in each.

Looking back, it is clear that we are indeed the sum of it all—the laughter, the tears, the silent moments, and the grand adventures. Each memory, each challenge overcome, and each joy shared has contributed to the rich, complex individuals we have become, bound forever by an unbreakable thread of love.

As we gaze upon the path we have traveled, hand in hand, I am filled with gratitude for every moment we have shared, for the love that has been both our journey and our destination. At the end of the day, and along the way, our love remains the greatest marvel of all, a testament to the enduring light of our union.

Thank you, my love, for being my companion, my confidant, and my heart's truest friend through every season. As we stand in unison, reflecting on our life together, I am overwhelmed with love, gratitude, and a deep, abiding peace, knowing that we have lived well, loved well, and are, truly, the sum of it all.

With all my love, for all our seasons and beyond,

Yours, in everlasting love and unity. Charles

Autumn's Close: A Shared Journal Entry

November 29th

Her handwriting:

As the last leaves of autumn surrender to the ground, making way for the first whispers of winter, I find myself reflecting on the journey we've embarked upon together. Each leaf, a memory; each breeze, a whisper of the times we've shared. The world outside prepares to slumber, but within us, a fire burns ever bright, a testament to the warmth we've nurtured in the heart of the coming cold.

His handwriting:

Turning these pages, our shared journal, feels like walking through a garden of our moments, each word a step, each sentence a breath of life we've lived. Autumn's departure is not an end, but a passage, a deep breath before the plunge into the introspective calm of winter. It's in this quietude that our love finds its deepest expression, in the silent watch of the nights lengthening.

Her handwriting:

Tonight, as we sit by the fire, I'm reminded of the promise of renewal that lies in the heart of every ending. This journal, filled with our thoughts, fears, and dreams, is a testament to that enduring cycle. As the year wanes, I see not a conclusion but a continuum, our love the thread that weaves through the seasons, unbroken and evergreen.

His handwriting:

And so, as we stand on the threshold of winter, I am filled not with trepidation but with gratitude. Gratitude for the autumn that has enriched us, for the winter that awaits, and for the spring that we know will follow. Our love, like the seasons, endures, evolves, and grows. It is the ember from which the new fire of spring will ignite a beacon through the longest night.

Her handwriting:

In the quiet that envelops us now, I find a profound peace. The kind of peace that comes from knowing you are exactly where you are meant to be. With you, my love, I am home. Let us step into the winter hand in hand, hearts joined, ready to face the cold, ready to welcome the light.

His handwriting:

Yes, hand in hand, with hearts ablaze, we step forward. The pages of our journal may pause, but our story continues beyond its margins, written in the frost that adorns the morning, whispered in the crackling of the fire, and celebrated in the silence of the snowfall. Here's to us, to our winter, to the love that warms the coldest days and brightens the darkest nights.

Seasonal Rituals

Her Journal Entry - The First Day of Spring

Each year, as the frost begins to recede, revealing the green beneath, we've nurtured a ritual to welcome the rebirth of the world around us. Together, we plant seeds in the earth, a symbolic act of our own growth and renewal. This year, we planted sunflowers, their faces destined to turn towards the sun, just as we turn towards the light in each other. This ritual, a dance with nature, mirrors the cycles of our love, ever-renewing, ever-flourishing.

Vulnerabilities and Triumphs

His Letter to Her - After a Summer Storm

Last night's storm, fierce as it raged against our windows, found us huddled together, your hand in mine. In that moment of vulnerability, with nature's fury around us, I felt an overwhelming sense of triumph. Not over the storm, but within us. Our love, a shelter in the tempest, has weathered much, standing resilient through every trial. It's in these moments of vulnerability that our love shines brightest, a beacon of triumph against the darkest skies.

Looking Forward

Shared Vision Board - The First Snow of Winter

As the first snow blankets the world in silence, we sit together, not with words, but with images and dreams, creating our vision board for the years ahead. Pictures of places yet to see, goals yet to achieve, and simple moments we yearn to share, adorn this board. It's a mosaic of looking forward, a tangible representation of our dreams, laid out before us. This ritual, amidst the quiet of winter, is our promise to keep dreaming, to keep looking forward, hand in hand, into the future we'll create together.

Making It Interactive

Their Interactive Anniversary Book - Compiled During Autumn

For our anniversary, we've created something special—an interactive book filled with memories, letters, and prompts for future adventures. It's a living document of our love, with pages left blank for the moments yet to come. There are envelopes to be opened on future anniversaries, each holding a letter or a challenge—a dance class, a night under the stars, a recipe to cook together. This book is not just a recount of love; it's an invitation to keep living it, deeply, joyously, together.

Spring: The Promise

Her Diary Entry:

The day we met, the cherry blossoms were in full bloom, a canopy of pink against the crisp spring sky. In that moment, under their gentle watch, a seed was planted in our hearts. The cherry blossom, with its fleeting beauty, became our symbol—a reminder that while moments are transient, memories are eternal. Each petal, a promise of the love to grow, as fresh and vibrant as the spring itself.

Summer: The Flourish

His Letter to Her:

As summer unfolds, the memory of cherry blossoms lingers, like a sweet perfume in the air. It reminds me of us—how, from the promise of spring, we've flourished. Our love, like the sun-drenched days of summer, is full and resplendent. Though the blossoms have faded, our love stands in full bloom, rich and enveloping, a testament to the growth we've nurtured in the warmth of our affection.

Autumn: The Reflection

Their Shared Journal Entry:

Autumn arrives, and with it, the memory of cherry blossoms feels both distant and near. The trees stand bare, their branches a stark reminder of seasons passed. Yet, in their silhouette, we see the promise of renewal, of cycles that turn and return. The cherry blossom becomes a reflection of our love through seasons—a love that has deepened, its roots secure even as the world around us changes. Each fallen leaf whispers the tale of our journey, a reminder of the beauty we've shared and the depth we've discovered.

Winter: The Anticipation

A Letter from Her to Him, Tucked Away for Winter:

As winter cloaks the world in its silent embrace, the cherry trees stand silent, waiting. In this quietude, I find myself thinking of the blossoms that await beneath the snow, a hidden promise of renewal. Our love, too, awaits the spring, undimmed by the cold, a flame that warms the heart of winter. The cherry blossom, now a memory, becomes our beacon of hope—a reminder that after the longest winter, spring will return, bringing with it the bloom of our love, renewed and radiant.

The cherry blossom, recurring in its cycle of life, becomes more than a motif; it is a narrative thread that binds their love story, a visual echo of their enduring bond. In its delicate beauty and cyclic nature, it mirrors the phases of their relationship, a symbol of their love's resilience and capacity to bloom anew with each passing season. This motif deepens the narrative, inviting readers to see the beauty in each moment, the promise in every ending, and the joy in awaiting new beginnings.

3. Interactions with Nature:

In the story of their love, the natural world becomes a silent witness to the ebb and flow of their emotions, the growth and challenges of their bond, and the renewal that each season brings. Through their interactions with nature, the landscape around them becomes a mirror, reflecting the internal journey of their relationship in its myriad forms.

Spring: Awakening

In the tender light of spring, they walk hand in hand through fields awash with new blooms, the earth soft underfoot, the air filled with promise. Here, in the rebirth of the world around them, they see the reflection of their own beginning—a love fresh and burgeoning, full of potential. The gentle uncurling of leaves, the brave push of flowers towards the sun, echoes their cautious optimism, the tentative steps of their hearts towards each other.

Summer: Flourishing

Summer finds them lying together in the lush grass under a canopy of green, the world around them vibrant and full of life. The sun warms their skin, and the gentle buzz of insects fills the air—a testament to the abundance of the season. Their love, like the summer, is radiant and assured, basking in the warmth of its prime. The lazy flow of rivers and the rustle of leaves in the breeze speak to the deep, comfortable currents of their bond, a love that has found its pace, steady and sure.

Autumn: Deepening

As the world dons its mantle of reds and golds, they wander through the crisp air, hand in hand, watching as the world transforms. The falling leaves, with their burst of color before the end, mirror the deepening of their love—a love that has grown richer, more complex with the passage of time. This season of change reflects the challenges they have faced, the inevitable shifts in their journey, and the beauty that lies in resilience, in the willingness to let go and trust in the renewal to come.

Winter: Reflection

In the quiet of winter, they stand together on a blanket of snow, the world around them hushed and still. The stark beauty of the bare trees against the winter sky speaks to the essence of their love, stripped to its core, resilient in the face of cold challenges.

The silence of the snow-covered landscape mirrors the peace they have found in each other, a deep, abiding calm that comes from facing the storms together, from finding warmth in the cold. It is in this season of introspection and rest that their love finds its strength, ready to burst forth anew with the spring.

Through each season, their interactions with the natural world around them not only highlight the beauty and impermanence of the external landscape but also delve into the evolving narrative of their love. This constant dialogue with nature enriches their story, providing a vivid backdrop to the dance of emotions, challenges, and joys that define their journey together. In the reflection of the seasons, their love story unfolds, a testament to the enduring cycles of growth, challenge, renewal, and the eternal promise of spring.

Family Gatherings

Their home becomes a haven for family gatherings, where meals are shared around a large oak table, stories and laughter echoing off the walls. These gatherings are a testament to their love, a space where it can expand, touching the lives of siblings, parents, and children. Through celebrations and trials, the couple's relationship serves as a cornerstone, a source of stability and love that ripple outward, strengthening the bonds of family.

Community Engagement

Together, they engage in community projects, from revitalizing the local park to organizing charity events. Their love inspires action, a shared commitment to making the world around them a better place. This involvement weaves them into the fabric of their community, their relationship a model of partnership and cooperation. As they work alongside their neighbors, their love is both a silent witness and an active participant in the collective endeavor to nurture and support the communal space.

Impact on Others

The narrative introduces secondary characters whose lives are touched and transformed by the couple's love. A young niece, inspired by their devotion, learns the value of commitment and kindness. A long-time neighbor, witnessing their unwavering support for each other through health scares, finds the courage to reconnect with estranged family members. These stories of influence and impact serve to highlight the expansive nature of love, how it can inspire, heal, and connect, extending far beyond the confines of a single relationship.

Shared Challenges and Triumphs

The story also delves into the couple's shared challenges and triumphs with their family and community, showing how these external relationships test and ultimately strengthen their bond. Facing a family crisis, they lean on each other for support, their love becoming a beacon for others in dark times. Celebrating community victories, their joy is magnified by the collective happiness, a reminder that love is not just an emotion to be hoarded but a gift to be shared.

Legacy of Love

As the narrative unfolds, it becomes clear that their greatest legacy is not in the tangible achievements or the events they organize but in the quality of love they embody and share. Their relationship becomes a living lesson in compassion, resilience, and the transformative power of love, leaving an indelible mark on their family and community.

In the warmth of their home, where laughter resonates like a melody and the aroma of shared meals fills the air, their love becomes a beacon, drawing family together in a celebration of unity and affection. The oak table, a sturdy witness to these gatherings, holds stories spilled over cups of tea, secrets whispered under the hum of conversation, and the silent, strengthening threads of familial bonds. These moments, rich with the essence of togetherness, are the couple's legacy, a testament to a love that nurtures not just two hearts but a whole family.

Outside the sanctuary of their home, the couple steps into the wider world, where their love extends hands to their community. The local park, once forgotten, now thrives under their care, a green lung breathing life back into the neighborhood, a project that brought old and young together, working side by side. Charity events, infused with their passion and dedication, become milestones in the communal calendar, opportunities for connection, and acts of collective kindness. Their engagement weaves them into the fabric of their community, their love an undercurrent, inspiring collaboration, and camaraderie.

Through the seasons, their love story touches the lives of those around them. A niece, once shy and uncertain, finds inspiration in their unwavering support for one another, learning the value of kindness, the importance of laughter, and the courage to dream big. A neighbor, estranged from family, witnesses the couple's journey through health scares, their solidarity in the face of adversity a silent encouragement. Moved by their example, he reaches across the chasm of years and misunderstanding, extending an olive branch to his own family. Their love, in its quiet strength, becomes a beacon of hope, a catalyst for reconciliation and healing.

Together, they face challenges, their love a fortress against the storms of life. When illness shadows their door, they stand united, their bond a source of comfort not just to each other but to their wider family, showing that love, in its essence, is the greatest healer. In moments of triumph, their joy is amplified by the chorus of their community's celebrations, a reminder that happiness shared is happiness multiplied.

As the years weave their story into the fabric of their family and community, the couple's legacy emerges not in grand gestures but in the simple, everyday acts of love and kindness. It's a legacy that inspires, a love that transforms, proving that the most profound impact we can have been through the way we love and support each other. Their journey together becomes a blueprint for their family, a guide for their community, showing that love, in its truest form, has the power to change the world, one heart at a time.

In the end, as they stand hand in hand, looking back on a life well-lived, they see not just the path they've walked but the lives they've touched, the mountains they've climbed, and the storms they've weathered. They marvel at the sum of it all—their love, a masterwork, woven through the tapestry of countless lives, enduring, inspiring, and infinitely beautiful.

5. Historical or Cultural Backdrop:

In the heart of the Scottish Highlands, during the turbulent years of the early 18th century, our tale unfolds, where the wild beauty of the land mirrors the fierce and passionate love between, a weaver's daughter with the soul of an artist, and a young bard with the heart of a rebel. Their love story, set against the backdrop of the Jacobite risings, becomes a testament to the enduring power of love amidst the chaos of history.

Chapter IV: In the Shadow of Ben Nevis

As the first light of dawn crept over the rugged peaks of Ben Nevis, painting the glen in hues of gold and purple, Elspeth and Callum met in secret, beneath the ancient rowan tree that had witnessed their love blossom from the tender shoots of friendship. The world around them was ablaze with the whispers of rebellion, the air thick with the scent of unrest. Yet, in each other's eyes, they found a haven, a quiet resistance against the turmoil that threatened to engulf their land.

Chapter VII: A Weave of Love and Duty

In the warmth of her father's workshop, Elspeth wove tartan, the threads intertwining as intricately as the path of her own heart. Each pattern spoke of her love for Callum, a silent prayer woven into the fabric of her clan. But society's expectations weighed heavily upon her, a mantle as oppressive as the English laws that sought to erase her heritage. Her love for Callum, deemed unsuitable by her family, became a symbol of defiance, a challenge to the cultural and societal norms that sought to dictate their fates.

Chapter XII: Ballads of Rebellion and Heart

Callum, with his lyre and his voice, became a beacon for the Jacobite cause, his ballads stirring the hearts of those who dreamed of a Scotland free from English rule. Yet, his songs also spoke of a more personal battle, a yearning for the freedom to love without restraint. In hidden glens and moonlit fields, he sang of his love for Elspeth, a melody that became a rallying cry for those who dared to dream of a world where love knew no boundaries.

Chapter XVIII: The Siege of Fort William

As the Jacobite forces laid siege to Fort William, the reality of war tore through the Highlands, a brutal reminder of the cost of freedom. Elspeth and Callum, caught in the crossfire of history, found their love tested as never before. It was in the midst of this chaos that they made a vow, beneath the shadow of the fort's walls, to stand together, come what may, their love a beacon of hope in a world engulfed by darkness.

Epilogue: The Legacy of the Glen

Decades later, the tale of Elspeth and Callum, immortalized in the ballads that Callum once sang, became a legend in the glens and valleys of the Highlands. Their love, having weathered the storms of conflict and societal expectations, emerged as a testament to the enduring power of the human heart. The rowan tree, under which they had whispered vows of eternal love, stood tall, its roots entwined with the history of the land and the legacy of a love that transcended the boundaries of time.

Set against the rich historical and cultural backdrop of 18th century Scotland, Elspeth and Callum's story is not just a tale of love but a narrative that explores the depths of human resilience, the fight for cultural identity, and the unyielding power of the heart to find its counterpart, even in the face of overwhelming odds.

In the rolling hills of Wales, where ancient castles stand as sentinels over the lush valleys, the love story of Sognia, a miner's spirited daughter with dreams larger than the mountains themselves, a poet with a revolutionary's heart, unfolds. Set against the backdrop of the Welsh Revival at the turn of the 20th century, their tale is a poignant exploration of love's power to transcend societal upheavals, cultural renaissance, and the quest for identity.

Chapter IV: Under the Watch of Snowdonia

Beneath the imposing gaze of Snowdonia, painted with the first light of dawn, Charles and Sognia shared stolen moments in the shadow of ancient yew trees. The air around them buzzed with the energy of change, the valleys echoing with hymns of revival and whispers of independence. In each other's presence, they found peace, a quiet rebellion against the external pressures that sought to shape their destiny.

Chapter VII: The Tapestry of Heart and Heritage

In her father's modest cottage, Sognia crafted tapestries that told the stories of Wales, her fingers deftly weaving the legends of old into vibrant images. Each piece was a testament to her love for Charles, threads imbued with hope and defiance. Yet, the expectations of her community, rooted in tradition and the harsh realities of life in the mining towns, loomed over her, casting a shadow on her love for Charles, deemed unsuitable by her kin for his revolutionary ideas.

Chapter XII: Verses of Change and Love

Charles, with his pen and his passion, became a voice for the Welsh Revival, his verses a beacon for those who dreamt of a Wales reborn, free from the yoke of industrial toil and cultural assimilation. His poetry, however, was not just a call to political action but a declaration of his love for Sognia, a promise of a future where love could flourish, unchained and unbridled, in the hills and valleys of their homeland.

Chapter XVIII: The Struggle for Eisteddfod

As the national Eisteddfod approached, embodying the cultural and linguistic resurgence of Wales, Charles and Sognia found themselves at the heart of the struggle, their love a microcosm of the larger battle for Welsh identity. The festival, a celebration of Welsh arts, literature, and music, became the backdrop for their most profound challenge yet. Amidst the poetry, the music, and the fervent display of national pride, they vowed to forge a path together, against the odds, their love a testament to the enduring spirit of Wales.

Epilogue: The Legacy of the Valleys

Years later, the love story of Charles and Sognia, enshrined in the folk songs and tapestries of Wales, became a legend, whispered in the same breath as the tales of heroes and dragons. Their journey, marked by the fervor of the Revival and the struggle for cultural preservation, emerged as a beacon of hope, a reminder of the power of love to inspire, to challenge, and to endure. The ancient yew trees, under which they once whispered their vows, now stood as guardians of their memory, entwining their story with the soul of Wales.

Transposed to the heart of Wales, Charles and Sognia story becomes an emblem of the Welsh spirit—resilient, passionate, and deeply rooted in the land. Their love, set against the turn of the century's cultural reawakening, reflects the universal quest for identity, freedom, and the unyielding bond that ties us to our heritage, making it a timeless testament to the power of love amid the tides of change.

Chapter IX: The Hearth's Whisper (Sognia's Mother's Perspective)

In the warmth of our kitchen, where the hearth whispers tales of old, I've watched my Sognia grow from a girl dreaming by the fire to a woman whose tapestries speak of our land's soul. And then came Charles, with his fiery words and dreams as vast as the valleys. Through a mother's eyes, I saw two hearts intertwine, challenging, supporting, and enriching each other. In their union, I witnessed not just the merging of two spirits but the awakening of a collective hope—a Wales reborn, not just in song and story but in the very fabric of love.

Chapter XV: The Oak Under Snowdonia (The Meeting Spot's Perspective)

Centuries I have stood, rooted deep within the shadow of Snowdonia, a silent sentinel to countless tales of joy, sorrow, and love. Yet, there is a tale that whispers with the wind through my branches—a tale of Charles and Sognia. Beneath my boughs, they shared secrets and dreams, their laughter and love carving memories into my bark. Through seasons of change, I bore witness to their love—a love that, like my leaves, blossomed anew with each spring, a testament to endurance, a promise of renewal.

Chapter XXI: The Voice of the Valley (Charles Friend's Perspective)

I've known Charles since we were naught but lads, running wild through the valleys, our hearts as untamed as the land. When he met Sognia, I saw a shift, a purpose kindled within him. Through his eyes, I learned of love's power to inspire, to drive us towards dreams we dared not dream alone. Together, they became a beacon for us all, their love not just a private joy but a public declaration, a rallying cry for a Wales that held fast to its heart, its language, its very essence. Their love story, interwoven with the cause of our land, reminded us that in love, as in life, there is always a cause worth fighting for.

Chapter XXX: The Echoes of Eisteddfod (The Festival's Perspective)

For generations, I have been the soul of Wales, a gathering of hearts and minds, a celebration of our cultural spirit. Yet, in the year of Charles and Sognia vow, I became something more—a canvas for their love. Their story, imbued with the essence of the Welsh revival, pulsed through the throngs of poets, musicians, and dreamers, igniting a fire that would burn long after the festival's end. In their love, I found my true purpose not just to celebrate Welsh culture but to embody the resilience, the passion, and the depth of connection that defines it.

Through these alternate perspectives—the watchful eyes of a mother, the ancient wisdom of a meeting spot, the camaraderie of a lifelong friend, and the collective soul of a cultural festival— the narrative of Charles and Sognia love expands, offering a kaleidoscopic view of its impact. Their love becomes a conduit for exploring broader themes of identity, cultural resurgence, and communal hope, painting a picture of a love that, while deeply personal, resonates with universal truths about the power of connection to inspire change and nurture a collective spirit.

7. Artistic Elements:

In the woven narrative of Charles and Sognia love, artistic elements—sketches, poems, songs, and recipes—become the milestones marking the journey of their hearts and the heritage they cherish. Each piece, a testament to their affection, infuses the story with a depth of emotion and cultural richness, rendering their love not just in words but in the very fabric of their shared life.

Charles's Tapestry of the Valley

In the early days of their courtship, Charles gifts Sognia a tapestry that captures the essence of their valley. Woven into the fabric are the hues of the Welsh hills at dawn, the vibrant greens of spring, and the golden warmth of the setting sun against Snowdonia. This tapestry, a visual love letter, hangs in their home as a constant reminder of their roots and the beauty of the land that shaped them.

Charles Poem: "Heart of My Heart"

In a moment of inspiration, drawn from the depth of his love for Sognia, Charles pens a poem titled "Heart of My Heart." The verses speak of two hearts beating as one, of a love as enduring as the mountains that cradle their homeland, and of a promise to walk the path of life together, no matter where it leads. This poem, shared at the national Eisteddfod, becomes a symbol of their commitment, echoing in the hearts of all who hear it.

Their Song: "Cân y Cariadon" (Song of Lovers)

Together, by the hearth on a winter's evening, Charles and Sognia compose a song that weaves their individual stories into a harmonious melody. "Cân y Cariadon" tells of their journey through the seasons, of challenges faced and overcome, and of the joy found in simple moments shared. Sung in the Welsh language, it becomes a staple in their family gatherings, a melody that binds them to each other and to their heritage.

The Recipe: Cawl Cariad

On a cold winter's night, Sognia prepares Cawl Cariad (Love Stew), a hearty dish made from lamb, leeks, and root vegetables, simmered slowly over the fire. This recipe, passed down from her grandmother, is infused with memories of family and warmth. As they share this meal, it becomes more than sustenance—it's a ritual of care, a symbol of the warmth and comfort they find in each other's presence.

These artistic elements—each tapestry, poem, song, and recipe— serve not just as milestones in Charles and Sognia journey but as artifacts of their love, each carrying a piece of their story, their dreams, and their heritage. Together, they form a unique, personal touch to the narrative, illustrating the many ways love can be expressed and remembered, transcending the limitations of time and space to capture the eternal in the ephemeral.

Charles Poem:

"Heart of My Heart"

In valleys deep where ancient echoes play,
Beneath the watch of mountains, stern and stark,
There, in the dance of night and break of day,
I found you, love, the heart of my heart.

Through seasons' turn, where fields of heather bloom,
Beside the streams that sing of olden tales,
Our spirits met, dispelling gloom,
With love as vast as Wales.

In every verse, my soul's confession,
A melody of hope and fear,
Your love, my guiding star, my lesson,
In every word, you near.

So, hand in hand, let's forge our path,
Through storm, through sunshine, joy, and wrath.
For you are mine, and I am thine,
Together, love, in endless rhyme.

"Cân y Cariadon" (Song of Lovers) – Lyrics

(Verse 1)
In the heart of the hills, under whispering stars,
We tread paths of old, our stories to tell.
Hand in hand, with the night as our witness,
In the song of our hearts, together we dwell.

(Chorus)
Oh, my love, in the dance of the dawn,
In the silence of snow, where our promises born.

Through the valleys we roam, with our hearts as our guide,
In the song of our love, forever we'll abide.

(Verse 2)
Through seasons of joy, through tempests of trial,
Our melody soars, over mountain and vale.
With each note, in the cadence of life,
In the harmony of love, we will not fail.

(Chorus)
Oh, my love, in the dance of the dawn,
In the silence of snow, where our promises born.
Through the valleys we roam, with our hearts as our guide,
In the song of our love, forever we'll abide.

(Bridge)
In the whispers of wind, in the murmur of streams,
Our song will endure, like the fondest of dreams.
For as long as the sun greets the land with its light,
Our love will remain, our future bright.

(Chorus)
Oh, my love, in the dance of the dawn,
In the silence of snow, where our promises born.
Through the valleys we roam, with our hearts as our guide,
In the song of our love, forever we'll abide.

The Recipe: Cawl Cariad

Ingredients:

- 1 lb diced lamb shoulder
- 4 large potatoes, peeled and cubed
- 2 carrots, peeled and sliced
- 2 leeks, cleaned and sliced
- 1 large onion, chopped
- 1 turnip, peeled and cubed
- Handful of fresh parsley, chopped
- Salt and pepper to taste
- Water

Instructions:

1. In a large pot, brown the lamb over medium heat to render out some fat.
2. Add the chopped onion to the pot and sauté until translucent.
3. Fill the pot with water until the ingredients are well-covered, bringing it to a boil.
4. Reduce the heat to a simmer, adding the potatoes, carrots, turnip, and leeks to the pot.
5. Season with salt and pepper, and let the stew simmer for at least two hours, or until the meat is tender and the vegetables are cooked through.
6. Just before serving, stir in the fresh parsley for a burst of flavor.
7. Serve hot, with crusty bread on the side to soak up the broth.

This traditional Welsh stew, shared with love, embodies the warmth and comfort of home, a dish that Charles and Sognia would have enjoyed on many a cold night, surrounded by tales and the soft glow of the hearth.

Music enthusiasts:

Creating a Melody for "Cân y Cariadon"

1. **Choose a Key**: For a song that embodies both the beauty of love and the resilience of the human spirit, consider a major key that offers a bright and uplifting sound. D major or G major could be fitting choices, providing a warm and inviting tonal landscape.

2. **Determine the Time Signature**: A time signature of 4/4 is traditional and versatile, suitable for both verses and choruses. However, for a more lilting, folk-inspired feel, you might explore a 3/4 time signature, which can lend a waltz-like quality to the melody.

3. **Compose the Melody**: Start with the chorus, as it's the heart of the song. Aim for a memorable, singable melody that captures the emotional core of the lyrics. Use the natural rhythm of the words to guide your melody, allowing the stresses and flow of the language to suggest rises and falls in the musical line.

4. **Harmonize**: Add chords that support and enhance the melody. In folk music, simple, open chords often work best, creating a sound that's both rich and accessible. Consider using chord progressions that evoke a sense of journey and return, mirroring the narrative of love enduring through the seasons.

5. **Instrumentation**: For a song inspired by Welsh traditions, acoustic instruments like the guitar, harp, or violin can add texture and depth. The harp, in particular, could pay homage to the Celtic heritage of Wales, providing a delicate and ethereal backdrop to the melody.

Finding a Current Song for Tune Comparison

To find a contemporary song that resonates with the emotional tone or structure of "Cân y Cariadon," look for tracks in the folk or indie genres, as these often prioritize lyrical storytelling and acoustic instrumentation. Songs by artists like Mumford & Sons, The Lumineers, or Of Monsters and Men might offer the kind of emotive, narrative-driven melody that "Cân y Cariadon" seeks to embody. For example, "Little Talks" by Of Monsters and Men combines memorable melodies with rich storytelling, a modern echo of the traditional influences you might draw upon.

While creating the melody and finding a modern comparison, remember that the heart of "Cân y Cariadon" lies in its ability to connect listeners to the enduring power of love—a theme as timeless as it is universal.

A Leap into the Future:

In the gentle glow of twilight, the family of Charles and Sognia gathered in the old family home, nestled in the heart of Wales, where the hills whisper tales of old and the wind carries songs of the past. The room buzzed with the soft chatter of the next generations, children and grandchildren, whose lives were the living legacy of a love that had weathered the turns of a century.

Morgan, the eldest grandson, a young man with the fire of Sognia in his eyes and the gentle strength of Charles in his spirit, called for quiet. He stood beside the old fireplace, under the ancient beams that had borne witness to so much history, so much love.

"Tonight," Morgan began, his voice carrying a warmth that hushed the room, "we gather not just as a family, but as the bearers of a remarkable story. A story of love, resilience, and the power of dreams. A story that began with two hearts, Charles and Sognia, whose love became the cornerstone of everything we are."

He gestured to the tapestry on the wall, masterpiece, vibrant even as the years had woven their own tales into its threads. "In every thread of this tapestry, in every verse of the poems we know by heart, in the melody of the songs we sing, their love lives on. They taught us that love is not just a feeling, but an action— a choice to stand by each other, to build something greater than ourselves."

Aisling, Morgan's sister, stepped forward, her hands holding a worn journal, its pages filled with the stories, recipes, and sketches that had been passed down through the generations. "This," she said, opening the journal to a page marked by a pressed cherry blossom, "is not just a collection of memories. It's a blueprint for living, a guide to loving fiercely, to facing challenges with courage, and to never losing sight of who we are and where we come from."

The children, wide-eyed, listened as Morgan and Aisling shared tales of the Welsh Revival, of tapestries that whispered secrets of the past, and of poems that spoke of hope and defiance. They learned of Cawl Cariad, shared on cold winter nights, a recipe that was more than food—it was a symbol of warmth, of home, and of the enduring strength of family.

As the evening wore on, the legacy of Charles and Sognia was woven into the hearts of the next generation. Their love, a beacon through the years, inspired not just stories but lives lived with purpose and passion.

"We are the sum of their love," Morgan concluded, his gaze sweeping over the faces of his family, "a love that didn't just endure but thrived, shaping not just their future, but ours. Let us carry forward this legacy, living our lives with the same courage, the same love, the same hope. For in us, their story continues, a testament to the enduring power of love to change the world."

In the soft glow of the firelight, surrounded by the echoes of the past and the promise of the future, the family of Charles and Sognia felt the unbreakable thread that connected them—a thread of love, woven through the generations, eternal as the hills of Wales.

As the family's reflections on the legacy of Charles and Sognia began to wind down, the room grew quiet, a reverent hush falling over the gathered generations. It was then that Gertrude, Charles's mother, now nearing her centenary with a spirit as indomitable as the Welsh hills, stood. Beside her, Wally, Charles's father, his once fiery hair now silvered with age, but his eyes still alight with the wisdom and warmth of a life fully lived.

Gertrude, her voice strong despite the years, spoke first. "My dear lovelies," she began, her gaze sweeping over her descendants, "in your stories, in your songs, I hear the echo of a love that was once a mere spark between two young hearts under the canopy of our beloved Wales. That love, like the tapestry on our wall, has been woven into the very fabric of our family."

Wally, taking her hand, added, "That love was a beacon, a light that guided not just Charles and Sognia but all of us through times of joy and times of hardship. It taught us the value of perseverance, the strength found in unity, and the beauty of dreaming together."

Gertrude nodded, her eyes misting over. "But remember," she continued, "that the true measure of their love—and of any love, for that matter—is not just in the warmth it brings to our hearts or the challenges it helps us overcome. It's in the legacy it leaves, in the lives it touches and shapes long after the flame has passed from one generation to the next."

Wally squeezed her hand, his voice a tender echo to her own. "As you carry forward this legacy, let love be your compass. Let it guide you not just in the grand gestures but in the quiet moments—the simple acts of kindness, the patience in understanding, and the courage to stand up for what is right and true."

Gertrude leaned slightly towards the gathering, a matriarch addressing her kin. "Love," she said, "is the thread that binds us, the story that defines us, and the light that leads us home. Cherish it, nurture it, and let it guide you through the seasons of your own lives, just as it guided Charles and Sognia."

Wally, with a gentle smile, concluded, "And in that love, you'll find not just the story of two hearts but the story of us all—a story of resilience, of hope, and of the enduring power of love to create, to heal, and to unite. That, my dears, is the true legacy of Charles and Sognia, a legacy that lives on in each and every one of you."

As their words settled over the room like a soft blanket, the family felt a renewed sense of connection, not just to Charles and Sognia but to each other and to the generations yet to come. In the wisdom of Gertrude and Wally, they found not just the sum of a love story but the blueprint for their own lives, a call to live deeply, love fiercely, and carry forward the legacy of love that binds them all.

P.S.

In the rush of daily life, where the digital world often overtakes our reality, it's vital to remember the importance of stepping back, finding a quiet corner, and losing ourselves in the pages of a book.

This isn't just a luxury—it's essential nourishment for our souls.

The act of reading, of disconnecting from the incessant buzz of technology, allows us to recharge, reflect, and reconnect with ourselves on a deeper level.

So, make time to snuggle up with a good book; it's not an indulgence but a necessity for the well-being of your soul.

The core message of this collection of poems/letters/sonnets/stories:

The core message of **I LOVED YOU LIKE THAT! Winter, Seasons of the Heart – I Loved You Like That.** Resonates with the timeless truth that love, in all its forms, is the most powerful force in human life. It is a force that shapes destinies, forges connections across generations, and leaves a legacy that outlives the fleeting moments of our existence. Through the intertwined lives of Charles and Sognia, set against the backdrop of Wales's breathtaking landscapes and turbulent history, this collection reveals the enduring strength and resilience of the human heart.

Love, as depicted in the myriad forms of poetry, sonnets, and stories within these pages, is not merely an emotion but a journey through the seasons of life. It teaches us the importance of growth, the necessity of resilience, and the beauty of change. Each poem and story is a reminder that love's true power lies not in its perfection but in its ability to endure through challenges, to adapt, and to flourish anew with each passing season.

Moreover, this collection underscores the significance of heritage and the deep connections to the land and culture that shape our identities and our relationships. It celebrates the richness of tradition and the bonds of family and community, highlighting how these elements are integral to the experience of love and the legacy we leave behind.

Ultimately, "**Seasons of the Heart**" invites readers to reflect on their own lives, the nature of the loves they have experienced, and the legacies they wish to create. It encourages a deeper appreciation for the moments and the people that shape our stories, urging us to cherish and nurture the love that binds us, across time and beyond the confines of our own existence. The moral, then, is a call to live fully within the seasons of our hearts, embracing love's lessons and its gifts, for it is in love that we find our truest selves and leave our most lasting mark on the world.

Ending Poem:

"In Love's Eternal Garden"

Now at the journey's end, we softly tread
Within love's garden, where all seasons meet.
Reflecting on the path that we did wed,
Our hearts in gratitude, the tale complete.

For love, we found, is not a fleeting day,
But an eternal season, rich and deep,
Where every moment spent, in bright array,
Becomes the treasure that our souls will keep.

Through cycles of the joy, the pain, the growth,
We learned that love transcends the bounds of time.
A bond that, once forged, pledges both
To weather every change, to climb each climb.

So, take this verse, a key to unlock hearts,
And find within, the love that never parts.

Conclusion.

As the final page of **I LOVED YOU LIKE THAT! Winter, Seasons of the Heart – I Loved You Like That.** Turns, we stand at the threshold of understanding—a place where the whispers of the past meet the promise of the future. In the journey of Charles and Sognia, set against the resplendent backdrop of Wales, we've traversed the landscapes of human emotion, witnessed the resilience of love against the tides of change, and seen how deeply the roots of passion and heritage can entwine.

Their story, though uniquely theirs, speaks to the universal truths of love's power to inspire, to challenge, and to endure. From the first bloom of spring through the depth of winter, their love was both a sanctuary and a battleground, a testament to the belief that together, we are stronger, more vibrant, and more capable of facing the storms that life brings.

Charles and Sognia legacy, woven through the fabric of their community and passed down through generations, reminds us that love is not a momentary flicker but a flame that can warm countless hearts long after our own fires have waned. It is a call to each of us to live deeply, love fiercely, and leave behind a legacy that speaks not just of who we were, but of the love we shared and the lives we touched.

As we close this chapter, let us carry forward the lessons learned beneath the Welsh sky, holding in our hearts the beauty of each Season, the strength found in unity, and the courage to dream.

Let the story of Charles and Sognia be a beacon, guiding us back to the essential truths of our own hearts, reminding us that in the end, **love is the most powerful legacy of all.**

In their tale, we find not just a story of love, but a reflection of our own desires, fears, and hopes—a mirror showing us that the most profound journeys are those taken together, heart to heart, soul to soul, through the seasons of life. May their story inspire you to weave your own tapestry of love and legacy, rich with the colors of your own experiences, dreams, and passions.

I LOVED YOU LIKE THAT! Winter, Seasons of the Heart – I Loved You Like That is not merely a book to be read; it is a journey to be lived, a reminder of the enduring beauty of love through the ages. As you move forward, may you find, like Charles and Sognia, that love is not only about the joy of the bloom but also about the richness of the harvest, the peace of the winter's embrace, and the eternal promise of renewal.

In this story, as in life, love is the enduring melody that calls us home, guiding us through the Seasons of our hearts.

To ALL the loves of my life. And the ones who've loved me back.

Reflecting on all the loves of one's life, including those who have loved us back, is like wandering through a gallery of the heart, where each relationship is its own portrait, filled with colors, textures, and emotions unique to the bond shared. Whether these loves have been fiery and passionate, gentle, and nurturing, fleeting, or enduring, each one holds its place in the tapestry of our lives, contributing to the person we become.

1. The First Love: Often youthful and idealistic, this love teaches us about hope and heartbreak, setting the stage for all that follows. It's a tentative step into the vast world of emotional connection, leaving an indelible mark on our hearts.

2. The Passionate Love: This love is intense and all-consuming, a whirlwind that sweeps us off our feet. It's the kind of love that feels like a storm, full of electricity and energy, teaching us about desire, loss, and sometimes, the hard lessons of letting go.

3. The Unrequited Love: Not all love is returned in the way we hope, but even unrequited love shapes us. It teaches resilience, the value of self-love, and the courage to face rejection, helping us grow stronger and more compassionate.

4. The Companionate Love: This love is a gentle, steady presence in our lives. It's built on deep friendship, mutual respect, and an unwavering support system. This love teaches us about loyalty, shared dreams, and the beauty of a quiet, steadfast connection.

5. The Transformative Love: Sometimes, someone enters

our life and changes everything. This love reshapes our world, altering the way we see ourselves and our future. It's a catalyst for personal growth, inspiring us to become better versions of ourselves.

6. The Lasting Love: This is the love that endures, weathering the storms of life together. It's a testament to the power of commitment, understanding, and forgiveness. This love teaches us about the depth of partnership, the joy of shared history, and the peace of knowing you are truly seen and valued.

7. The Self-Love: Equally important is the love we cultivate for ourselves. This journey teaches us about acceptance, the importance of setting boundaries, and the strength that comes from recognizing our own worth.

Each of these loves, along with those who have loved us back, contributes to the richness of our lives. They teach us, challenge us, and support us. They show us the depths of our capacity for love and remind us of our inherent worthiness of being loved in return. As we move through life, these relationships are the milestones that remind us of where we've been, who we are, and the endless potential for love that resides within us.

About the Author

MGM Meddis, a name synonymous with compelling storytelling, is a critically acclaimed author whose narratives have captivated readers worldwide. Residing in the picturesque landscapes of the Golden Horseshoe, on the Shores of Lake Ontario, Canada, her surroundings provide an endless source of inspiration, breathing life into the characters and settings of her tales. With an impressive repertoire that includes the psychological depth of "By Reason of Insanity" and the sensual allure of "Forbidden," MGM has established herself as a formidable voice in literature, her works available for the eager reader on Amazon, and wherever fine books are sold.

A woman of intriguing complexity, MGM invites us into her world, offering a glimpse of her private and natural essence, a facet of her being that demands acknowledgment by anyone who wishes to truly understand her. Her intellectual journey was uniquely shaped by private tutelage under a family friend, a university professor, whose guidance enriched her formidable mind.

After a successful and dynamic career in the corporate sphere, where she achieved her professional aspirations, MGM chose to pursue her true passion, dedicating herself to writing full-time. Her versatility as a writer is evident in the wide array of genres she navigates with ease, from thrillers and drama to romance, fantasy, children's stories, and poetry. As she continues to explore the vast landscapes of human emotion and imagination, readers worldwide wait with bated breath for her upcoming releases.

For those drawn to the depth and diversity of her storytelling, MGM's journey and works can be explored further at her website and social media.

Here, in the realm of her creation, every reader can find a story that resonates, a narrative that whispers directly to their soul.

Keep an eye on her evolving body of work, for MGM Meddis is an author whose tales promise to leave a lasting imprint on the world of literature.

Other Books by Mgm Meddis

FORBIDDEN

BY REASON OF INSANITY

ETERNAL ECHOES

ECHOES OF ABSENCE

HEARTSTRINGS & TIMELESS TIDES

WHISPERS OF ETERNITY

I LOVED YOU LIKE THAT!: *Spring, A tapestry of Love.*

I LOVED YOU LIKE THAT!: *A Summer's Journey*

I LOVED YOU LIKE THAT: *Autumn, Grateful Hearts.*

I LOVED YOU LIKE THAT!: *Winter, Season of the Heart*

ECHOES OF LIGHT

ECHOES OF THE UNBRIDLED

LUMINOUS THREADS

VOICES OF THE HEART

A TRIBUTE TO HIM

WHISPERS OF THE HEART

YOU ARE THE WRITER

Table of Contents